Renegotiating the Church Contract

*The death and life of the
21st-century church*

JAMES THWAITES

paternoster
press

Copyright © 2001 James Thwaites

First published in 2002 by Paternoster Press

08 07 06 05 04 03 02   7 6 5 4 3 2 1

Paternoster Press is an imprint of Paternoster Publishing,
PO Box 300, Carlisle, Cumbria CA3 0QS, UK
and
Box 1047, Waynesboro, GA 30830–2047, USA
www.paternoster-publishing.com

British Library Cataloguing in Publication Data

A catalogue record for this book is available from the British Library

ISBN 1–84227–098–2

Cover design by Campsie
Typeset by Waverley Typesetters, Galashiels
Printed in Great Britain by Omnia Books Ltd, Glasgow

Contents

Don't blame me if you don't read the preface

If you quickly browse this book, as many are in the habit of doing to books, you might well gain the initial impression that it is yet another tome firing cannonballs at the beleaguered church, taking pot shots at the besieged pastor therein. Another angry man with an axe to grind, you might say, as you place it back on the shelf. I could well imagine such a response to the contents of this book from the browsing public. However, if one looks more intently, or perhaps turns to the last few chapters of this book and reads, one will, I believe, be surprised at the extent of support given to the church gathered and to the role of ministry gifts.

As I will argue, the church construct that presently houses most of the people of God is not something separate to us to be left at the side of the road in our rush to the postmodern. Rather, it is an expression of the way that we, as Christians born and bred in the West, think. To leave the church as construct behind and walk away is to deny much of what is real about each one of us. To react is to carry the same thinking that formed much of our present way of being church with us into the future.

It is generally agreed, by most of the people who inhabit the pulpits or the pews, that the church is in trouble. It has reached an impasse. It is simply not succeeding in its work of penetrating the earth with kingdom salt, good leaven and divine light. My intent in the pages to follow is not to simply state again the problems most all know are there. Rather, my desire is to move through to a resolution of this impasse that we, as the church, are presently facing. My desire is not to tear down the buildings, forsake the gatherings and send the pastors and priests packing. Instead, I believe that we need to track with the church gathered and with leadership to see change come. We need to search for a new way of being church in which we can place these and other God-given resources strategically and effectively. Before we do that, however, we need to work through the impasse. If this does not happen we will succeed only in rearranging the furniture once again.

To my mind for this impasse to be breached there needs to be a thorough evaluation of the way in which platonic dualism and platonic idealism have influenced the nature and structure of our present way of being the church. Platonic thinking has caused us to build a way of church that has become bounded within a construct, a company or, in some instances, a corporation. As a consequence, we have predominantly defined the church as something distinct to the people that make for it. We have identified it mostly with the meetings, the leaders and the programmes within the construct. By so doing, we have substantially taken it away from people and consigned it to a subculture that is unable to deeply penetrate the world with the light of the gospel. We did not set out to do this, but this is what has happened time and time again down through the centuries.

It is this way of being church that many believe has now reached a dead end. God is at work to bring this 'construct' into death. To do this he has to bring those identified with it into what might be called a time of 'divine dying'. This book is about the history and nature of that construct. It also seeks to track the journey of transition that the people of God need to take through death and into new life at this time. It does this by looking at the incarnation of Christ from the perspective of his engagement of the power structures, both earthly and angelic, of his day.

To analyse a part of a thing and then express that analysis is to exaggerate it. The reason for this is that in an analysis you have to necessarily spend more time on certain aspects of a thing than on others. Hence, one tends towards generalisation in any observation or critique. Such is another challenge with the examination that follows. There are many different kinds of motivations, people, approaches and circumstances. To speak of one so as to highlight a particular issue is to appear to disregard or not take into account another. In the pages that follow I will not be attempting a thorough examination of all churches everywhere – perish the thought! Rather, I will, as mentioned, be going after what might be called the platonic virus, with a view to tracing the course of the infection it has caused to the body of Christ, the church. In this I will, of necessity, need to be selective in the use of my magnifying glass.

There is a church I know of and have worked with in England that to my mind represents the middle bandwidth of the current situation. I hope, among other things, that by using this example at the outset I might convey the impression that I am aware that life is never simple and church life is even less so. This might put me in better stead when later on, to demonstrate a point, I draw examples from settings that are more obvious or extreme. In this church there are many good people doing great things. There are business people, folk working in the home, healthcare workers and others, all finding it hard, sometimes very hard, to cope with the juggling act called life. Like many church leaders of late the elders and ministers of this congregation have moved away from the single man at the top to more of a team ministry approach. Alongside this they have also sought to lessen the sense of there being some kind of strong ruling centre over people and process. They are seeking to release more of the saints into their own life and work and, like most, wondering what it will take to keep the youth in the church loop.

As the leaders have sought to do this they are coming under a whole new set of pressures. There are those in the congregation with a busy life who simply want a good church with a clear vision and strong centre to do things on Sunday and during the week that fulfil what they see as the kingdom mandate. These are not as happy with the blurring of the centre and the lack of vision they see in the seat of church authority. There are others who welcome the greater affirmation they have of late received in regard to their own work. However, this initial move to more affirmation has not been followed up by very much change in the level of support, resource and teaching they get in relation to their work. For these working people it still seems that the church as construct is, as ever, the place where the real ministry is done and the eternal action takes place.

As one worker said to his church leader: 'Even though your brochure says that you support us in the work we do in life, seeing it as our calling and our ministry, the perception still comes across that the church, defined by its meetings and ministers, is primary and we, the everyday workers, are outside of that loop.' The church leaders plead for more time to catch up, but find that the pressure to deliver in line with past contracts or patterns of church are still strong and keep them too busy to decidedly build something new. Like many fellowships the church has started cells in the hope that this will in part solve the dilemma they face. The plan is that each of these will take on a mission and thereby further decentralise the church. This move has helped, but for most leaders and the 'laity' who look to them, the change is still incremental and not enough to encompass the complexity and pace of post-modern life.

When these leaders attempt to release the saints into their life and work by changing the culture of church they come under pressure to keep the church the way it has been. When they set out to equip the saints to salt, light and leaven their world they find themselves limited by the constraints of a bounded church culture. There is a conundrum at work here, one that is not all that simple to define or unravel. What is it that these leaders are up against? Can they resource those in the world of work while keeping those wanting church the way it has been happy? How can you properly direct something if you take away a strong sense of central leadership? Here in this example I believe we are seeing the birth pangs of something new. We are seeing a conflict between holding and release, between construct and creation, between an old way of being church and a new way trying to emerge from that old.

A group of leaders came together to pray in relation to a congregation of around 150. One of the leaders present said in relation to the meeting, 'We were praying with some power for an outward focus by the church. As we did this we sensed a resistance, not so much demonic, but rather a mindset. One person described it as a "wall that we did not break through". The congregation leader called it a mindset that needed to be broken. This breakthrough, he said, was critical to the release of the people of God into the future. Others saw it as "X" painted on the wall of church, a no-go area that they had, to date, not considered to be their main problem. On that day it was marked for further action.'

If we are to make it through that 'no-go' area and engage the creation that calls our name we need to look again at the church contract we as leaders and laity have signed. We need to trace the lines of platonic code in the programming that has formed our way of being church.

We need to track the threads of platonic dualism and idealism that have shaped the underlying thinking on which our way of constructing reality, and particularly church reality, is founded. There needs to be a dying to a way of being church that derives from platonic dualism and idealism. Again, through this time of transition all of the good things of gathering, of worship, of leadership and more are not to be forsaken, rather they are to be found anew and valued afresh in the life that emerges from this time of dying.

A new landscape is opening up before us at this time, a new landscape served by a theology of church that enables us to see Christ's body living and working with impact in every sphere of creation. If we do not deal with our present thinking in relation to the church as construct, then we will not be able to clearly see and thus effectively engage the creation as the church as fullness. The truths concerning death, transition and new life, drawn from the incarnation event, need to first have their effect in the household of God. From there these principles can be taken into every sphere of creation to see the powers overthrown and the life and fullness of Christ's body the church, spoken of in Ephesians 1:23, arise.

So, there it is, the well-tensioned and the pointed, the strong statements and the more balanced, the hope for the future and the pain and dying we need to go through to get there. I do hope you find these in good measure and of some help in the pages to come. In, through and over all that follows I pray that we, Christ's body the church, will go through this transition – for the sake of our children, for the sake of the creation and for the sake of our eternal Father and his eternal Son.

www.newlandscape.net
www.beyondtc.com.au

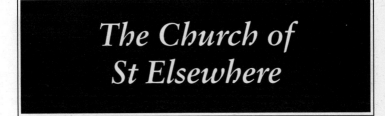

*The Church of
St Elsewhere*

Chapter 1

Fishing for a Future

It's like every church in London has a sign on the door saying 'gone fishing'. So said the leader of a church movement with regard to the present state of play. By the way, the word 'fishing' here is not a reference to evangelism. Another well-known leader said recently that he was no longer sure he believed in the local church – a remarkable statement from a person who has spent decades planting them. It was as if the queen had said she no longer believed in the aristocracy. Others speak of the generational handover from founders to followers, with the next in line uncertain of what they are supposed to do with the people being entrusted to their care. They are unsure of how the old fits into the new because they do not know what the new looks like. All this is not to say that nothing good is happening. New programmes of outreach are having their impact, people are being cared for and nurtured, and worship and prayers offered to God. However, it appears that the environment in which these and other good things occur is becoming more and more blurred. There is a growing fuzziness afoot, both in the midst and at the edges of the local church domain.

A part of the current church wobble, particularly in those streams that tend towards the charismatic end of the spectrum, relates to the build-up and let-down that has happened in the past five to ten years. The expectation was that recent moves of the Holy Spirit in refreshing and renewal would result in the lost being found in increasing numbers in the local church on Sunday. The immense energy and hope invested in this outcome, now apparently stalled on the rocks of reality, has dispersed into emotions of disappointment and intensified the general feeling of malaise. Other developments, coincident with the above moves of the Holy Spirit, relate to the church strategy side of the equation. This came initially with a call for local churches to come together in unity and prayer. This very positive move saw Anglican and Catholic, free church and Pentecostal/charismatic talking and praying together like never before. It helped to shift the focus of many away from congregation building to city taking. In addition, there was a growing emphasis on the need for reconciliation of past wrongs and a stronger emphasis on prayer and intercession. Much, however, of these essential developments in church thinking and strategy were taken up in the later part of the 1990s and fuelled the expectations of revival.

The more evangelical part of the spectrum experienced mixed fortunes during this time. Many in the traditional church were surprised as society began to get over some of its reaction to Christianity and began to consider the church again. Their church schools began to fill as parents decided that Christian teaching could be of benefit to their children's personal and career prospects. Outreach courses like Alpha spurred many a church fellowship into action and helped precipitate a renewed interest and response to the gospel among the unchurched. Of interest here is the Alpha programme; it was more successful in the traditional churches than the charismatic streams.

That being said, the signs from the traditional side of the church equation were not all good. Many of these churches still struggled, with a number going out of existence as their constituents moved away or grew old and passed on. Surveys spoke of thousands each week deciding to no longer attend church, half of these being under the age of eighteen. Ministers held on Sunday to Sunday, week to week, faithfully preaching the Word to keep the faithful fed. However, the church as a cultural alternative still failed to impress a society driving past on its way to work, shopping, sporting events or some other leisure activity. With the slow-down of charismatic growth and more attention being paid to some of the more traditional churches by society, some of those more traditional churches felt better than they had during the 1980s. However, the problems that beset them from before the time of charismatic emergence still remained to be addressed and overcome.

Returning now to the more evangelical/charismatic part of the church equation. The revival expectation hit a peak around 1998. After that time and into 1999 it became evident that the expected breakthrough had not occurred. Instead, saints in these settings found themselves turning up for the next Sunday service on the calendar, looking at their pastor as he took them through that more contemporary order of service once again. In their leader's eyes many caught a glimpse of sadness, even remorse, arising from another season of hope deferred. This, as is the lot with the leader, was well masked by courage and the vision thing. But those close enough to their pastor, or those in leadership, knew that this time the build-up/let-down had taken much, if not most, of the wind from the sails of the church vessel. This time around they knew that they could not return to the same old meetings. It was at this time that more saints decided to join many of their post-evangelical friends on a fishing trip.

On the banks of the river, some involved in the 'saints gone fishing' fellowship began to see a stirring in the waters.

They had been in meeting after meeting for years and years and had now taken time out to think. The stirring in the waters was a stirring in their hearts. It was a move of heart desire that dared to think that perhaps it was their life, their work, their wanting from within that now should find expression. Mixed in with this was a frustration with their leaders, along with love and respect for all that they had contributed to their lives over the years. In certain cases this frustration had turned to anger, even to out-and-out rebellion, or it had spiralled down into confusion, tinged by depression. Some leaders rushed to corral these emotions back into the church stable, unable or unwilling to see them as being the first steps in a journey to locate the heart that had for years beaten strong in hope of life – a life that their local church experience had prepared them for, but had not been able to give. These saints believed they had waited long enough for the local church to deliver on its promises. Their life was passing by and they could wait no longer.

Individual saints began to think that perhaps Christian life belonged to them, to their friends and family, to their work and their city, and was no longer going to be a subset or asset of the local church. With uncertain faith, sketchy theology and cautious hope, some began a journey. Sometimes the leaders of their congregations understood the shift in these people's lives, but as pastors they were reluctant to overly bless what they did not understand and as yet could not fully trust. Other saints made the move without reference to their pastor or church. Deciding that because the answer would be a theological or political 'no', they would not bother to ask the question. It also needs to be said that an increasing band of pastors began to imagine their own escape plan at this time. In their dreams they could see themselves asking the members under their charge 'If you leave me, can I come too?'

Authority moves

Two other things happened at this time, after which this simplified account of a complex situation will close. On the church strategy side of things there was a progression from city orientation towards a focus on 'the land'. This was assisted by moves to reconcile and fathom history by addressing the sins of the fathers and the redemptive/creation purpose of nations. This move was also served by the emphasis on creation theology/spirituality, awakened by a re-evaluation of such things as Britain's Christian Celtic heritage, the Eastern Orthodox tradition and the Hebrew worldview.

The second significant move that took place, soon after revival expectation was dashed, was a shift in certain sections of the church towards stronger authority and corporate structures. This happened in subtle and overt ways. It was more noticeable in nations like America where idealism and the corporate model of church are favoured. However, it was by no means limited to that nation or to those nations more strongly influenced by the pattern of church that America generally promotes. In other less corporate-styled streams leaders, sensing that the church boat was rocking too far to the left (taking in water and losing too many over that side), began in a more subtle way to beat the loyalty drum. Their motives were no doubt mixed, but perhaps many sensed that disappointment might lead to a scattering of the troops and hence moved to rally them around the flag again.

What was noticeable, again more in the American setting (but this particular setting, to my mind exemplifies in a more obvious way thinking and practice that exist in the church globally), was the move to invest more authority in the apostles. At this time (early 2000), one prominent US teacher informed a conference crowd that he believed anyone leading a congregation of over 700 was an apostle. He went on to say that if your fellowship was smaller than that number, then you should locate an apostle in your area and begin to orientate your ministry and church life towards his leadership. Such a shift should remind us of the move towards the rule of bishops in the fourth century AD. However, the environment at this time was calling for greater security and the leaders were in the mood to give it. Thus, the needs of the present took precedence over any memory of the past.

Creation or corporation

On one side we see a move towards the creation and on the other a move towards the corporation (stronger regulatory authority), both trends appearing at the end of a five/ten-year build-up and let-down phase. The situation is of course more complex than this. In the current climate there are many in the confused middle, uncertain of whether to go in the direction of the creation or the corporation. Many do not know that these two alternatives are opening up before them at this time. Also there are many, sitting in supposed safety, who still do not know how confused they are! Among these are people whose life has taken the seat of judgement on what they see as the Pentecostal/charismatic tendency towards the high and presumptuous. The only movement detected here are lips declaring that the present low in the charismatic movement is well deserved. However, those whose refuge is in their creed or their reaction fared no better during the decade. Their reluctance to believe that God might move in a way that would turn the tide did not necessarily spring from faith. This is to say that the passion of those church streams and individuals that reached for more in God and more from God is to be honoured. I do not want to give the impression here that I think it was entirely misplaced. Again, in my observation, the trend to creation or corporation (with apologies for those who cannot tolerate generalisations) seems to be evident. Why at this time are these two options presenting themselves to us?

In essence they have always been there, but in the present climate they are becoming more visible to us. This arises from several winds of change. Firstly, the growing emphasis on creation theology has given us eyes to more clearly see the extent to which we have been held back from creation engagement by the present bounded culture of church. The Hebrew vision of creation – one that sees the church as God's people living and impacting in every sphere of creation, placing the gathering in a servant rather than master role – is offering a theological alternative to the present congregation-focused ecclesiology (doctrine of church). Underlying all of this, the church's quickening journey to cultural oblivion is helping us to concentrate our thinking concerning the future like never before.

In effect, we can no longer afford the luxury of the present set-up. The local church is a threatened species. Will it continue to head into larger well-organised game parks to preserve its culture or will it head into the creation to find its inheritance? Could it be that God gave us what we wanted in these past years, more to show us our hearts than to win the lost? What kind of church culture would we have brought these many thousands of newly saved sons and daughters into if revival had come? It is one thing to fill a building with people; it is another thing altogether to release sons and daughters into creation to find their inheritance. I do not believe we are capable, under our present culture of church, to accomplish the latter.

Could it be, as one leader said in relation to the recent moves of refreshing and renewal, that 'God is offending our minds to reveal our hearts'?

Core issues at the church soul

Many people believed that the past ten years of build-up and progression would finally result in the reinvigoration of the local church so that it could continue to be the centre from which the kingdom radiated. I do not believe that such is the case. My conviction is that these years have brought out into the open the strongholds that are at the heart of the issues that keep us from the divine purpose in creation – that being the issues of authority and control that reside at the heart of the present church structure. I believe that God is answering prayers that have pleaded for the release of the body of Christ into the earth. He has always wanted our light to fully shine, our salt to strongly savour and our leaven to mightily work its way through the lump of earth under our feet. Also I believe that the developments in our understanding of the things of the Spirit and of church strategy in the past decade have not arisen to serve the local church or even the cell movement. Rather God has brought these to light to equip the sons and daughters to engage all of the created order.

This issue, to my mind, is the critical one that God is setting before us at this time. From the time of the fourth century to this day we have not really changed our theology of church. The local church has been the centre and focus for most all things Kingdom since that time. The Reformation accomplished much but did not really touch the issue of the rule and reign of the local church structure over the kingdom process. The local church as centre was first an expression of Rome's rule. Then, post-Reformation, it was an expression of the states' control. Then, post evangelical awakening, of the denomination's institutional oversight and now, in the Pentecostal/charismatic stream, we have the pastor/leader as Chief Executive Officer (CEO), essentially mimicking the corporate world. The church as construct continues to sit, as it has done for centuries in one form or another, at the centre of God's people and God's purposes.

The moves to cell are good, but in most instances the process is still highly engineered and regulated by leaders from the centre. Certainly I do not want to take away from this expression and strategy. However, to my mind this wineskin, though better suited to move people into the new season, still defines the church primarily as meeting (now in homes); rather than seeing it as being the saints in all of life, work and relationships in creation. Saints are still not encouraged, or in some instances not permitted, to cross over and identify in a primary way with other networks (say related to work or other initiatives) and streams (other denominations) outside their particular camp of meeting. Cells are still deemed to arise from a cultural centre that is identified with a leadership that regulates and sets the boundaries of that culture. Also, the genius of the G12 strategy (discipleship groups of twelve people where each person disciples twelve and on from there), if used essentially to build the local, mega or cell meeting culture, will over time come under the same spell as most other innovations used to keep the status quo in place, i.e. the dominance of the meeting, culture and the leader's management over the kingdom, people and process.

I have noticed that some people have moved their churches into cafés. I have noticed that some people have hacked out the pews and brought in little tables and chairs. I wonder if we have changed the way the church actually is. Have we changed the way we are being church together or just the way we sit together?

Cathy Kirkpatrick, Mark Pierson and Mike Riddell,
The Prodigal Project, p. 45.

Choice time

I believe that the rise in the authority agenda that we are now seeing gives us an opportunity for choice, the likes of which we, the church, have not had for many centuries. On one side there is the choice to decidedly and radically release the sons and daughters into creation. On the other side, a choice, as church leaders, to keep the saints under our social and spiritual control, regulating and managing them via gatherings of different shapes and sizes under our leadership.

If the church continues to be governed by the same authority structure and thinking that has been in place (in one form or another) since the fourth century, then it will not make it into the creation to find its identity and gain its inheritance. If we continue to regulate from our power base the kingdom people and determine from our church/apostolic centre the kingdom process, then nothing will really change. We might embrace cells, G12, Hebrew visions of creation and market-place ministry, but if our present way of exercising authority over the people and the process remains, then the same old ideology will continue to reign.

The local church, cell-based or otherwise, is at the centre of this drama. It currently holds most of the saints in its weekly orbit. What it decides about its future will, to say the least, be telling. I believe that the present local church construct can no longer survive in its present form unless it succumbs to the pressure to move towards the stronger corporate-styled expression of church. At first this statement might appear as a contradiction to the general thrust of my argument. What I am referring to here is that the average local church, getting weaker within and uncertain of the way ahead, will need to become more like the stronger corporate-styled churches (not necessarily in terms of numbers, but in ministry philosophy) or it will decline.

Remember the church situation I wrote about in the preface? Here the move to release the saints was being increasingly met by a move to shore up the church centre by giving it a strong vision and a clear mandate. Of course there will be exceptions to the process I am describing. However, I believe that the average local church will find it increasingly difficult to sit in the muddled middle. This observation is drawn from those nations where the corporate form of church is in place. These churches offer a stronger, clearer, more secure definition of being Christian and being church. In a complex world saints are increasingly being drawn to such settings. What this means is that those leaders who desire to release the saints to be the church in all of life will face resistance and the need to pay a cost to get there.

The wash around the church tub these past years has now flushed to the surface the issue of authority like never before (in the past century at least). The move towards leaders taking a stronger headship over the church is now clearly emerging. It is being presented as the way to go, the only route for the church to take if it is to impact society and come into its inheritance. Because the middle ground is becoming more and more untenable, this simpler authority push will exercise an increasingly stronger pull in the years ahead. In this trend, God is, I believe, presenting leaders with a choice – to release the saints into creation or to keep them within the church as construct or corporation.

Some may feel that strong authority centres with strong release of the people can go hand in hand. I am aware that some structures are so strong that they can afford to release some. But even here the psychological/spiritual/ authority centre these people are tied to will only permit them to go so far and no further. At the end of the day such measured releases will not accomplish the divine strategy. They may let out some steam and lessen the frustration, but if the name church is kept tied to the leader's centre, then the saints will continue to remain as members of the church of elsewhere and the cry of creation will remain unanswered. Many will hope to have it both ways, a strong centre and a strong release, but the church as centre will, as it has done for many centuries, win every time.

My belief is that the authority move will get stronger before David is ready and, Saul-like, this stronghold falls on its sword. The Word says that judgement begins in the household of God. This means that divine reality comes to bear down on the sons and daughters in a stronger way first before that reality rolls out into the world at large. Right now the divine reality check is well under way. The thoughts and intents of many hearts are up for review.

A time to die

If the name church is to name all of the life and work of the saints, then something in our present way of being church must die. The generational stronghold that controls the people and the process, a stronghold established by the platonic worldview, must be taken into death. This will not simply be a matter of a local church deciding to jump from the old to the new with a six-week sermon series, a market-place cell or two and some conferences on work. Nor is it a matter of saying that the problem of authority and control only happens in larger corporate-styled churches. The truth is that such thinking resides in every heart and every social grouping. It is only when our authority is challenged or threatened that we come to really know our heart in the matter. It is one thing for one's authority to be threatened by something evil. That is something that leaders can generally deal with. However, at this time it is being challenged by people wanting release, by creation demanding that reality come from the body, by society increasingly disregarding the social structure we call church and ultimately, in and through all of this, by our Father wanting his sons and daughters to emerge to fill creation and gain their inheritance.

The only way to transition from old to new is to allow the local church to go into the divine dying. Whether we like it or not, this is what is now happening. The church, as we have known it, is dying. Its spiral in certain streams into authority and control mode is a very clear indicator of this (as much as it is an option, as it were, given to draw out our heart and clarify the choices we need to make at this time). We have a choice to enter into divine dying leading to life or a destructive death with no future. I am perhaps over polarising; God is kind as he is severe. It is in his hands what he will do in relation to this person and that leader. That being said, it is important to stress here in closing that we cannot hope to simply and easily go from old to new in this journey. Like any good and divine thing, the journey into new life must go into and through the dying of Jesus. Unless a grain of wheat fall and die it will not spring into life and bear the fruit God intends. Whoever gets the name church wins. This is a very political statement I know, but one that needs to be made. The name church is the one that the gates of hell will not prevail against. It's the most powerful name ever given to humanity. The stakes for control of it are high indeed. To begin our examination of this church let's take a journey into it and try to fathom what makes it tick the way it does.

Chapter 2

What is This Thing Called Church?

Remember the 'no-go' area, marked with an 'X' that appeared during that meeting I referred to in the preface of the book? Let's go there now by asking the question: What is a church? Strange question, you might say. Mostly it's strange because we, like many of the people in that meeting, have to date neither been inclined nor in many instances permitted to ask it. We have, for the most part, taken it for granted that a church is in fact a church! But more and more saints are daring to enquire down that line. What they are after as an answer is as yet unclear, but there is a stirring in their heart that tells them something is not right. There is a desire they have for life and reality that is moving them to question the basic assumptions embedded in the text of their weekly church newsletter. I received this e-mail the other day from a fellow in the Midlands of England. It expressed well the growing angst in the pews.

The internal discomfort of the elders

'I am an Elder in the church. My "church" ministry is preaching/teaching – I speak around once a month on average. I am also in full-time "secular" work. I have been with the same company for thirteen years and have risen through the ranks to a position where I now have some influence/authority. My wife is a "five-star Christian", we have three children; our oldest is soon to go off for a further two years to Bible school, our middle child is soon to leave school and hopes to go onto a Christian music school for a year before seeking to serve the Lord full-time in music. Finally, our youngest is going on with God and has a heart for caring for people. Everything is great! So why do I feel so ill at ease? Why am I so frustrated with church?'

One of the ways to enter into possible answers to the question 'what is a church?' is to look at how they start. Forgive the obviousness of the following, but my hope is that in this we will perhaps begin to see what, to date, has not been obvious.

A person (call him Tim) with his wife (call her Sally) decides to start a church. Tim studies and gets ordained and one day they both head out to find a building. After a few months of praying and searching they settle on one. It's just an average building, a part of an office complex in an industrial part of town, but it's the church premises they have been looking for. The next phase, with a little help from their denomination and their core team, is to lay the carpet, install the sound system, build the office, get the seats in place and organise the first Sunday service. Before Tim conducts this first meeting, he has to get a vision statement that will inform people that his new church is not only contemporary, but is also on the move to somewhere great. Pastor Tim, as he is now called, settles on the well-known vision to 'Know God and make him known'. This he puts on every brochure alongside the name he has had in mind for many years, that being 'Harvest Community Church'.

The time is now at hand. With pulpit installed, offering bags purchased, overhead projector positioned, musicians under control and core team briefed, they are ready to do church. And sure enough on the first Sunday in May, with 17 adults and 2 children in attendance, Harvest Community Church begins. A month later there are 36 adults and 5 children at church, then another month passes and it's 24 and 2, then next month it's 40 and 7. On and on these numbers and Sundays roll through the years of programmes, crusades, cells, renovations, leadership team shuffles and the rest. Ten years on, the first Sunday in May comes around once again. It's time for an anniversary celebration. In attendance there are 140 adults and 18 children. During that decade a tremendous amount of energy has been expended to bring these people together in a room several times each week. The struggle and sacrifice for Tim and Sally has taken its toll on both of them. There have been two church splits during the decade and only a few of the original committed core remain to celebrate the victory. And what is that victory? It is the existence, the ministry and the people named 'Harvest Community Church'.

What could be the problem with all or any of this? Well, I could start with the obvious things like: this form or way of being church is not reaching our society with the kingdom. In fact the culture of our society is doing a far better job reaching and winning the people in our churches. I could speak of how congregations like these make for the denominations that, as representative of the Christian church, are being pushed ever out to the cultural margins of society. I could point to the hard reality of literally thousands of traditional congregations in the Western world now fighting for their survival, adding that even community-based Pentecostal/charismatic churches, because of intensifying market warfare with the mega-churches and the charismatic catch-up of the evangelicals, are now beginning to face a similar struggle to that of the more traditional congregations. The reason why I won't go in that direction is because I feel that much of this external reality has most to do with the day-to-day reality happening inside Pastor Tim's church. One can blame postmodernism, the mega-church competition or the internet for local church demise, but my feeling is that the reasons are far closer to home than we have, as yet, given ourselves permission to think.

The makings of a domain name

To cut to the quick here: What do I think is the problem with what Tim has done and is doing? The key issue, to my mind, is that Tim has applied the name church solely to the activities he conducts within and from his building. In so doing, he has created a distinct ecclesiastic 'domain'. He has done this by drawing a social and psychological circle around a set of activities managed and overseen by himself and calling the things inside that circle 'church'. Tim has made a distinction between his 'domain' and the rest of what the saints are and do in life. He has assumed the right to name what he does 'church' and by implication has not permitted the saints to name what they do as 'church'. Hence the name, against which Jesus said the gates of hell would not prevail, has become contained in an organisational construct supervised by Pastor Tim.

I am aware that many pastors would preach that the people are in truth the church. But in reality it is more than evident that the local church considers itself to be church proper and church central, with the people of God gathering in and going out from it. The local church sees itself existing at the centre of the divine strategy, as the primary place from which the mission of the church is launched. As an indication of the centrality of the local church domain, any Christian ministries that do not have a congregation attached to their activities have no right to be called church. Rather, they are given the rather quaint name of para-church. They are considered to be subsidiaries to the main player, which is the local church. Individuals ministering apart from the local or para-church entities are given the title 'personal ministry' to describe where they fit in the kingdom scheme of things. The local church holds the authority, the finances, the titles and the keys of the king-dom in this age. This arrangement is so well entrenched in our thinking and practice that we take it for granted. However, we can no longer afford the luxury of doing so.

The marriage of church and culture

The second thing that arises from what Pastor Tim has done relates to a very powerful thing called culture. Tim has been busy for ten years making his church culture the dominant culture of the people who attend. He has worked hard and long to make his church culture one with that of the Christians who identify with him as leader. The way in which he conducts his church programme, what he preaches about or permits to be preached, the things he personally endorses and backs financially are held out and promoted as being the primary culture from which the Christians who join get their bearings for life. We have all read, I am sure, some version of the following quote. It is from a church leadership magazine published during the year 2000 and reads: 'Ultimately each church will be a reflection of the personality of its senior leadership (pastor). You be what you want your people to be. We reproduce after our kind.'

Some might say in response to the above, 'Well, I certainly don't get my main bearings as a Christian from my church; only fundamentalists or charismatics do that.

The church influences me to a degree, and yes it has its place in the scheme of things, but it's not central to my life.' In answer, I do acknowledge there are different ways and degrees to which the Christian's personal culture interacts with their church's culture. This depends a good deal on the particular stream of church they identify with. Of course added to this influence will be their own experience of broader culture and their own choices in relation to both cultures. I would, however, argue that, no matter what the particular tradition or denomination, the church culture in every instance has a profound effect on the life of the Christian. For those who are more independent of their church (either by choice or in line with a church tradition that permits such independence) the way they live life is still very much influenced by what the church is and represents. How so?

Christians who live mostly apart from the influence of that church culture, cannot and do not (generally) lay claim to those 'sacred' things for themselves because the local church has taken to itself the right to conduct such things as the worship and preaching services, the rites and sacraments, the ordination of ministers, the directing of ministry activities, the collection of monies and so on. Hence their 'out there' life is characterised by the lack of these things. Most facets of their life remain 'outside' the church's domain, while other things in their life are designated as being 'inside' the ecclesiastic circle. It is in this way that the well-known sacred/secular divide enters in. Thus, even in these instances, the internal culture of the local church determines much of the external life of the saint.

The Pentecostal/charismatic and the stronger evangelical streams of the church are those that seek to mostly strongly preside over the way in which individual Christians conduct their lives. The Pentecostal/charismatic branch of the church is now calculated to be around a half-billion strong. As such it is now the largest single stream of the Christian church after the Catholic. In this stream to be a strong Christian is to be heavily involved in the local church. To be independent of the local church in one's actions or thinking, to live outside of pastoral covering, is to err. As such, the influence on the culture of those who attend is strong indeed – that being said, the impact that these churches have on their members it not really all that different from that of the older traditional churches. Your response to this assertion may be one of surprise, in that on the surface the opposite would seem to be the case. In support of this assertion let's look at more of the e-mail from the elder with the 'five-star Christian wife'.

The divided story continues

My background has shaped me into a rational reformed, 'lower-storey' Christian but I go to an upper-storey Pentecostal church. I have been amazed and not a little frustrated by the lack of focus on everyday life. I know of people in the congregation who find life a struggle. A number have fallen into sexual sin, others struggle with being single, still others have difficult marriages. Some women feel that the men treat them as second-class believers. Yet, despite all this, when we meet, we worship as if none of these issues existed! What recognition there is is limited to a short prayer at the start of the meeting. It's as if we want to get it 'out of the way' before moving onto the real business of the day.

Something has been eating away at me from within. It seems to me that, for the most part, today's church has removed itself from life, either through separation from sin/worldly passions and/or by its focus upon the meeting. Also, my sense of detachment comes, in part, from the feeling that I do not have permission to relate my work problems whilst at church. Yet my work takes up the vast majority of my life – why shouldn't it play a major part? Worse still, when I have sought help with work issues I have been advised to simply 'praise louder'! Needless to say I went away none the better for seeking help.

I find the church is slow to relate to 21st-century life. But this doesn't mean that the church is not active, just the opposite! We meet twice every Sunday and what do we do? Well, our first focus is worship and our second is the Word. There are also the notices for the next six-week programme of meetings! Sunday meetings, mid-week home group meetings, music practice, prayer meetings, youth outreach events, invite a non-Christian evening out meetings, drama events. Please forgive this overflow but, as you can see, I am wound up by the current situation.

The very intensity of the Pentecostal/charismatic culture has worked here to create the sacred/secular divide in the life of someone who is actually in the leadership of the church. The Christian is made to feel that most of their 'out there' life is a subset to the main action that happens in and from the church; the reason being that in these settings Christian life is tied up so strongly with church life. If the saint wants or chooses to live independently of the church, then she will have to more strongly negotiate with her church culture or decide to run all the more harder and further from its authority. In these settings living the 'out there' life is a hard call. In many ways it is more bereft of the sacred than is the case with older traditional church cultures. The reason being that so much more of the sacred is distilled and kept inside the church than it was in the older, more traditional churches.

The in, the out and the frustrated middle

There are people who are 100 per cent in the local church recipe, there are those who react and are on the run and there are those who dwell, like our elder friend, in the frustrated middle. Whichever way, the local church culture is the central player in the field these Christian people are trying to inhabit. It occupies a distinct ecclesiastic domain that functions as something 'other' to the saints. A whole lot is riding on whether the local church gets it right or gets it wrong because it holds in its leaders' hands the keys to the kingdom mission on earth. If the eternal purpose rises or falls on these local churches, then they need to be open, very open for an ongoing critique of the position they have chosen to occupy in the field of battle. My purpose in this analysis is not to be critical of the motives and actions of pastors who work and serve with integrity, love and sacrifice. Indeed, in my conversations with many church leaders, it is apparent that many feel trapped inside the present confines of their church premises. It is the ecclesiastic culture that they have inherited, the church contract they knowingly or unknowingly signed, that I am examining, not their motives or actions as leaders.

In this evaluation and critique of local church culture I will be concentrating more on the evangelical and Pentecostal/charismatic streams, on what is generally named the contemporary church, than on what is termed the traditional church. In this decision to concentrate on the contemporary church culture, I do not entirely exclude the older traditional churches. I have spoken of similar influences that arise from both expressions of church, indicating that the same thinking and practice defines and holds them both in their respective places. The reason that I will concentrate on the more contemporary churches is that they are more popular and thus more populated. Also they exemplify in a more obvious way the issues we need to address if we are to journey into the new landscape. It helps here to remember how radical most of the now traditional churches were when they first appeared. The reality is that the difference between the contemporary and the traditional is only one of degree and centuries.

In what follows, when I use the phrase 'local church' I will be speaking of the more contemporary-styled churches unless otherwise specified. Also, I will use the phrase 'local church', or 'church gathered', to describe community, mega and house church expressions. I am aware that there are differences between them, but essentially each sees the church gathered (in one form or another) and overseen by leaders as being the central, authoritative and culturally determining manifestation of the church on earth.

The local church has captured the name of church and the kingdom culture of the saints. By doing so it has created a sacred/secular divide in their life. A kingdom divided, as with a life divided, is ripe to be conquered. This, indeed, is what we have seen, both in relation to individual saints and also with regard to the institution of church. Hence the need to unlock this culture, work out why it is the way it is and fathom the thinking that holds its power in place. If we don't then we will find ourselves coming back to that no-go area several years on, with no change and even less hope than we have at present.

In conclusion here, Tim and Sally may or may not be aware of it, but they are in trouble. For all sorts of reasons related to their internal church culture and the external culture of the society they seek to reach, they are in a precarious place. If we are to draw the best from what they and others have accomplished and see it come through into the new, we will have to examine anew the underlying thinking that forms our way of being church. We need to look again at the local church's claims to central place in the kingdom purpose and question the nature of the authority it exercises over the life of Christians. We need to go past the no-go area painted on the walls of our local church buildings. We do this that we might carry the best of what is held within the local church into the new landscape now opening before us.

Chapter 3

The Power of Vision

It's a delicate matter to evaluate any culture, let alone the church culture. Tied into that culture is our understanding of who God is and, hence, what eternally matters. We are going in to appraise a place (environment) where many good things have happened over the years. It was there, on a Sunday evening three years ago, that someone's husband came to Christ. The healing of a friend during a conference in June last year, the dedication of a first child, the sermon that changed the direction of an entire life – these, and many other good things, happen in the church culture I am now going to critique.

Then there is the flipside of that golden coin – the pain of so much given to one's church over the years and so little appreciation returned; the devastation when the pastor fell into sin and left in a hurry; the arrival of the next big ministry trend, here today and gone tomorrow; the pain of the last church split, when a congregation was ruined because two elders had a titanic ego battle over who should be in charge of the building extensions; the time, money and passions given and given again and the uncertainty over where it all goes. These things also happen in the culture we are about to examine.

One can certainly experience a strange and wonderful life in the contemporary local church scene – the glory and the shame, the success and the failure, the sublime and the ridiculous are to be had therein. I believe the downside to the flipside of our golden coin arises not only from to-be-expected dysfunctional interactions between fallen people, but also from something that is amiss within the very culture of church itself. I mentioned in the prior chapter certain things that mark our present way of being church. There was the way in which people like Pastor Tim establish an authority domain called the local church, one that is separate or distinct from the rest of the life of the saints. This expression of the church then takes to itself the central and overseeing role in God's purposes on earth. Also we saw how the church culture sets out to become the dominant culture of the Christians who identify with it (or try and run from it!). Again, if this way of being and doing church has it wrong then both the lost and the found are infinitely and adversely affected; hence the need to carefully analyse the internal culture of the local church.

Foundational to this process of evaluation is the need to understand the impact of platonic/Greek thinking on our present church culture. I will use the word 'platonic' from herein to cover the entire set of influences on the Western world of Greek philosophy. I am aware that the Greek worldview is more than Plato, but, as he was particularly instrumental in introducing the dualism so foundational to Western thinking, his is the main influence and hence the name I will use to define the overall impact of the leaven of the Greeks.

The history of platonic influence is long and involved, and I will not try and cover it in detail. In the book *The Church Beyond the Congregation*, I examined in more depth the role of platonic philosophy in the development of the Western and Christian worldview. Much of what I am about to say is based on that treatment. For a more detailed examination of this worldview I would encourage you to read *The Church Beyond the Congregation* or any other book dealing with the platonic worldview. In particular I draw reference to Karl Popper's book *The Open Society and its Enemies. Volume 1. Plato*. This was a seminal book in the reappraisal of Plato's impact on Western thinking. It is a must read for those who want to wade more deeply into the foundational dogmas that influence human affairs.

The world of Plato

Plato said that the created world we see around us was not the real world. He believed that reality existed in a perfect state far removed from finite creation. In this realm the 'real' things and the perfect ideas were to be found. In our world we can only experience the faulty or lesser copies of these 'real and primary things'. What this means is that the things, people and events in creation are not the focus for truth or reality. Rather, meaning and purpose for life was to be found in a realm removed from this world. The platonic worldview, aligning with various religious and philosophical systems in vogue at the time, leavened its way into Christian thinking and overtook the early influence of the Hebrew worldview presupposed and taught in Scripture. Here follows an all-too-brief summary of platonic thought as contrasted with the Hebrew vision of creation.

- Platonic thought believes there is a spiritual realm that is separate and distinct from the natural/created realm. The Hebrews, on the other hand, saw the divine presence and word in, through and over all things of the present creation (Eph. 4:6; Rom. 1:20).

The Scriptures, of course, had primacy and authority in this creation-encompassing communication. For the Hebrew the spiritual (unseen) realm was one with the created realm.

- In platonic thinking heaven is identified with the eternal realm. It was deemed to be a plane of existence outside of space, time and matter. This belief caused the church to place heaven in its own distinct spiritual realm. It became something removed from the present life in creation and consigned to the after life. The Hebrews saw the heaven of God, his throne, existing over all of their life and work in the present age. The heavens and the earth in this age and the one to come are joined in space, time and glory; they are not and will never be 'spiritually' separated.

- Platonic philosophy held that conceptual/rational thinking was the key to accessing the perfect/ideal realm. Divine revelation and absolute truth were received only through conceptual or rational means, by 'pure thought'. The Hebrews were taught by God that truth is wisdom lived out relationally through good work in creation. It is the fruit of these good works and relationships that was the means by which the individual grew in relationship with and understanding of God himself (Col. 1:9, 10).

Which way does the vision look?

One of the single most strategic effects of the platonic worldview relates to the orientation it has given the church. Church culture does not head in the direction of the created order in its search for reality and for God because of the influence of Plato. Instead, it is perpetually on the move away from creation. Certainly the local church does endeavour to move the saints some distance into life. But rather than going in, through and over all things to grow up to the heaven above, it takes a sharp turn far too early in the piece and heads in a direction away from creation towards what it sees as the heavenly, eternal or 'real' realm. The consequence of this is that the present church culture, whether cutting-edge-contemporary or old-styled-sacramental, is, under the direction of Plato, heading in the wrong direction.

It is from this misdirected vision that all kinds of strategic errors arise. Rather than seeing people come to faith in Christ and 'grow up in all things' of creation through to the heaven above, the present church culture is mostly focused on saving people out of this world with a view to their entry into a heaven located in the next life. This heaven is not thought to be reached in, through and over the creation out there; rather it is held out as something mainly accessed through the 'in here' culture of church. This means that most people associate the spiritual/heavenly/eternal realm for the greater part with the things that happen in and from the local church setting. Saints are not taught to see and encounter God the Father 'in, through and over all things' of creation (Eph. 4:6). This means that their experience of God and of life is greatly diminished. The platonic set-up ensures that the saints individually and the church gathered are weakened and consequently the divine purpose is compromised.

Mixed motives, mixed messages, fixed agenda

As the flame is turned up and the light turned on to the platonic orientation of the local church culture, we can, I believe, begin to understand more about why this construct is configured the way it is. It helps us understand more about why Pastor Tim built his church the way he did. It follows that if the church has most to do with the 'spiritual' or 'truth' realm, then it must be something that occupies a separate/distinct space to the natural realm in which the saints live and work each day. Because of its orientation towards, and special access to, the perfect and eternal realm, it stands to reason that the local church would be deemed central to the process that moved people towards that realm. It then would appear to logically follow that the local church would have the right to set in place the culture of those it believes its authority and mandate cover. One might well wonder how differently this church might look if its platonic orientation were taken out of the way.

An uncovering of the platonic agenda enables us to understand more about why church is structured and oriented the way it is. It also helps us understand many of the otherwise elusive contradictions that are evident inside that culture. Why is so much of what the local church sets out to do not accomplished? Why are its designs so grand but its influence so bland? How can so many good pastors and preachers produce so few people able to impact their world? On these questions might go, each one indicating that something must be amiss. The harder the church works the less it seems to work.

The answer, or a major part of the answer to this conundrum, is, if we dare to look, there for us to see. I believe it follows this line of sight and logic. The local church, through its pastors, preaching and programme, does seek to empower the saints for life. In this endeavour it sets out on the right course of action. The problem is, however, that it does this ultimately with a view to seeing the saints, and the people they bring in, head in the direction the church is taking, which is away from that life. In this it appears to do one thing, but does it with a view to doing another. It is mixed in its motives, as it were, pulling the people this way and that, but mostly its way. And its 'way' has been predominantly set in place by platonic thought.

It is this understanding that I believe is a crucial evaluation tool for this time. If its logic and sight is applied to what is said and done in the local church, it can, I believe, enable us to untie the Gordian knot that binds us to the local church construct. The dysfunction and defeat we face owe much, if not most, to this contradiction and the confusion it brings to church life and strategy. As much as saints might try to swim (and ministers keep trying to teach them to swim) in the direction of the world to save it, all the time there is an undertow dragging them in the other direction, into the depths of the platonic illusion. If we do one thing with a view to doing the opposite, we are of all men most to be pitied! I will come back to the line of sight and logic again, but for now let's draw breath.

Take my breath away . . .

'Well, well,' said the man in the pew, 'it couldn't be as bad as all that, could it? I had a great Sunday last week, got blessed and challenged. My pastor is a godly man, works hard; visits if we're sick or missing. His preaching is fine most of the time. His leadership skills do leave a bit to be desired. He's more of a counsellor and teacher than a manager. Sure, no one has been saved for months and there is the usual drift of Christians in and out of this place on a whim and a fancy. Most people are so busy with work that they can hardly focus on the church programme anymore . . . OK, things are in a bit of a state. But, the way you have put it here, sounds like there's nothing happening at church. It almost sounds like we should not be thinking about going to heaven, and definitely we shouldn't be too involved in our local church. But, surely it must be a good thing to worship, to gather and hear the Word, what could be wrong with that? After all, there are some people getting saved, and besides, at the end of a busy week I like to go to church with my family. Are you trying to take that away from me?'

Yes, I have made a fairly dramatic incision here into the present culture of church. If one were to take a cross-section of a Sunday service one may not easily detect the kind of organism I am describing here. Others might take a sample and find it full of the culture I have described. Here I am drawing out into view the platonic leaven that has worked its way through the lump, unearthing the programming that has made its way into our church DNA.

Through what I have written, I certainly don't want to give the impression that the root of the church tree is all bad and that its DNA is fatally flawed. There is much that is good operating in our current church settings. The word, the worship, the gathering, the ministry gifts, the anointing and more are God-given and certainly give us life and power. It is these good gifts of God that we need to see come through all the more strongly into the new creation church.

I hasten to stress once again that I am not bringing into question the motives of leaders in making use of preaching, worship and leadership to build their local churches. To my mind they labour under the same platonic agenda that we all are burdened by. This is the lot that they have inherited. As such, blame levelled against them for the present way the church functions misses the mark by a long shot. God is certainly present in our times of gathering to bless his people, no matter what the influences at work therein. His presence and his blessings should not, however, be construed as a validation of all that is said and done inside the church domain. There is a great distinction between the good things that God has given us and the present way in which they are configured in the culture of the local church. Hence the need to make a clear distinction between what is viral and infecting his body, the church, and what is flesh and blood and thus intrinsic to its nature and purpose. Let's turn now to look at the nature of the platonic DNA and examine the code it has loaded into the church operating system.

Chapter 4

The Platonic Ploy

The platonic worldview did not come from God. It is not taught in Scripture. It should have no place in defining either the nature or the purpose of the church. Our challenge is that its leaven has worked its way substantially through what we deem to be the primary expression of the church – that being the local church organisation. Let's look at the main entry points of the platonic virus and seek to understand the DNA code it uses to take over healthy cells of the body.

There is quite some difficulty in describing something that does not exist or at best is unknowable. This is the challenge when it comes to examining the nature of the platonic regime. It is the unknowability or inaccessibility of the Platonic realm that is, as we shall see, the source of its power over so many people's lives. To uncover the reasons for its elusive sway over the Western and Christian minds we need to look into the way it taps into and turns the creation reality away from the good. Issues relating to the transcendence and immanence of God are our starting point. Transcendence refers to the person of God existing beyond the finite creation. Immanence speaks of the way in which God is revealed in a finite way in and through the creation. It is by creating confusion in our thinking between transcendent reality in God and our finite life in the immanence of God that Plato is able to gain such a powerful hold over our thinking.

We cannot directly know or experience the infinite God. This is why God made us in the immanence of the Son to know and be known by him (Gal. 4:9). As John said 'no man has seen God at any time; the only begotten God, who is in the bosom of the Father, he has explained (revealed) him' (Jn. 1:18). In the Son of God, in this life in creation, we are known by the Father and in that 'being known' we are able to grow up (in the immanence) in him through creation towards maturity and our eternal inheritance. The main point here is that the starting point for our understanding of and relationship with God is found in and through our life in the present creation.

The platonic Greeks, as we know, were not all that enamoured by the creation. They did not see it as a vehicle of revelation; rather they saw it has a hindrance. It was to them a dark, shadowy, corrupt, material illusion, obscuring one's vision of the pure, eternal and ideal realm. Is it any wonder they had neither the time nor the inclination to consider that truth and reality might be found in and through everyday life in creation?

Truth for Plato could only come from the transcendent realm – from outside of creation, time and the image bearer. So it was that this 'outside' realm became the focus of attention in platonic thought. The early Greek Christians didn't think twice about associating this eternally removed realm with the heaven spoken of in Scripture. For them heaven could not be a part of the creation. For it to be 'real' it had to be moved to the unsullied spiritual realm beyond time, space and creation. It was the removal of the spiritual realm from the natural realm and the dislodging of the third heaven (God's throne) from over creation into the transcendent that enabled the platonic agenda to triumph over the church.

Plato's power to deceive comes from the way in which he made use of the perfections (attributes, nature and power) of the eternal transcendent God. He made these the focus or the goal for human existence. There is a semblance of truth here, in that these eternal perfections do actually exist in God. But, as mentioned, they are infinitely out of reach. Things like the eternal, the ideal, divine holiness, absolute knowledge and the like exist only in the transcendent God himself. When the word 'perfect' (*teleios*) is used in Scripture in relation to our lives, it refers to our being who we were made to be. When Jesus speaks of being perfect like our heavenly Father is perfect he speaks of our journey towards the fullness of who we are, not a journey to arrive at the actual perfection of God himself.

Plato's ploy was to make the focus of life and truth something and somewhere outside the scope of human experience. He disconnected truth and reality from the life of the image bearer in creation and (supposedly) attached them directly to the infinite. Thus, rather than travelling in, through and over the finite revelation of God in creation, people were dislocated from their present life. Essentially what Plato has done in messing with our mind is to make us focus on the perfect and ideal rather than the good and created relational present. Our everyday life in creation is considered to be the backdrop, the waiting bay, the shadowland waiting for the defining moment when 'it' all comes into focus. The platonic realm is ever inaccessible to people because reality is always elsewhere – that being said, there are a group of people in the Platonic programme, the elite, who have special knowledge of this ideal realm. There are the chosen few who are in contact with the 'eternal'. These 'philosopher kings' and their role will be discussed further down the track.

The ideal within

For many centuries this ideal was found for the most part in a spiritual realm that was distinct from the created realm and only realised in the after life when you arrived in the Greek version of heaven. A shift happened in the Renaissance (fourteenth–fifteenth century) after a fellow named Aquinas, taking a cue from Aristotle, said that reality was also to be found in the things of the present life and could be known by rational thought. This could have been a step in the right direction; it did, in fact, deliver more dividends than the prior fixation with the other realm and the after life. However, people applied the same approach or philosophy of idealism to the present things of creation because platonic thought still very much held sway over the Western mind.

This meant that people began to relate to things in line with what they thought was the things' ideal purpose or perfect expression. The ideal expression of the thing was thought to exist within the ordinary (non-ideal) thing. The pursuit of this ideal still tended towards the old futurist orientation – in that the defining moment would see the ideal uncovered and thus be perfectly expressed. This way of relating is close to the creation purpose designed by God, in that there is a full finite realisation of glory to be found in each created thing. The attributes, nature and power of God do exist in every created thing, there to be drawn out and discovered by us – hence the subtlety of the platonic move. The trick comes in, as mentioned, in Plato's ability to get us to dislodge from the thing – whether it be the work, the relationship, the event or the physical thing – and move the focus of our thinking and living towards what we think is its ideal realisation in some other place or time. In line with Plato's belief that the perfect realm was accessed by 'pure thought', the conceptual or rational dimension came to the fore at this time. It was seen as the most pure and sure way to access the perfect within the relational/ physical realm.

God has called us to uncover the spiritual within the material, the unseen within the seen, the essence within the form, the eternal within the temporal and so on. Plato's departure from this creation purpose happened because he did not believe that the material, natural or relational realm was intrinsic or essential to that process of discovery. As distinct from Paul who taught that 'the spiritual is not first, but the natural; then the spiritual' (1 Cor. 15:46), Plato believed that the physical/natural realm obscured one's vision and encounter with the perfect/ideal expression of the thing. Thus, rather than travelling into the natural and relational realm to discover the attributes, nature and power of God, Plato dislodged people from the physical creation. He convinced us that the natural realm held no way through to the ideal spiritual or eternal realm. If we were to find our way through to truth, to reality, to God, we had to dislodge and detach from the illusion of the material and the present. So it was that after the Renaissance even the things of the present creation were captured by Plato, dislocated from what was real and relational, and their realisation or essence fixed to the ideal and perfect realm.

Another consequence of this present life idealism is that it ensured that the ideal within the thing or process became dominant over every other facet of it. This is seen in the Enlightenment obsession with reason as being the ideal essence within every thing or process. Once this 'ideal' was found and set in place then every other expression or dimension – the relational, moral, experiential, emotional and so on – was rendered subservient to it. This upshot of platonic thinking has had a profound influence on the way we in the West accumulate our knowledge and build our institutions. It sets up a psychological need to always have to find the key or the centre in almost everything we relate to. Once this key is found or this centre is located it then brings every other facet of the process under its jurisdiction. These other dimensions are then only able to contribute in line with the dictates of that which is ideal and thus central. The ramifications of this rule of the ideal are many and serious. So much of the tension and interactions of life that God intended for us were wiped out when rationalism came to rule the Western mind. So much freedom and creativity were taken away from people as the central and thus ideal power came to take charge of their life. To this day the tyranny of the ideal at the centre dominates the way we think, the way we organise our society and also the way we do church.

The ideal rule

This approach to life profoundly influences the ways people born in the Western world perceive and build their version of reality. People are programmed to think that the ideal marriage, the perfect place, the ultimate job, the best church, or the complete leader actually exists. Now frequently they tell themselves – or are told by the non-ideal part of the ideal thing they are fixated on – that this ideal is not and never will be real. But then they hear a story of break-through, they see a full-colour advertisement, they look at a brochure promising arrival, at another woman or man appearing to have an answer; and there it is, the elusive ideal is taunting them. The market place is playing with their mind again. So they resume their search for that other person/thing/event that will usher them into an ideal they feel must somewhere exist for them. In this obsession they devalue the present, put pressure on themselves and others to reach the unreachable and are driven to perform the impossible. Along this hard road they become prone to be controlled (and to control) rather than released to create and enjoy in regard to their life and work.

Idealism's ever-present mantra, designed to disconnect people from their own life and desires, is continually chanted over the airways, pushed in print media and preached from pulpits. It declares that reality is not you, it's not the place you occupy, it's not at this time, it's not the spotted desires of your fragile and fallen heart – it's somewhere, someone, something, sometime other. It's when you are strong enough, when you are pure enough, when you have enough, when you die and go to heaven. It's when you rise to fame, when you own this, when you can do that, when you are like this – whatever, it's just not you, it's just not here and it's just not now. And because it's not you it must come from elsewhere. It might be the product you purchase that allows you to identify for a few hours with the celebrity that endorses it. It might be the church you attend where you can identify with the dynamic leader who has special access to the realm ever beyond you. It might be the body of knowledge you must have to give your life the (ideal) definition you need to break through or at least feel secure. It might be the anointing that will one day come, if you have enough faith to deserve it. It might be a perfect moral state that you will one day attain to if you keep thinking, adjusting and performing the right way.

Until the time that the ideal arises to conquer your present half-life, you need to keep taking the cure, keep performing, keep trying, keep giving, keep attending, keep obeying. Don't ever give up, because one day you will be 'there'. And where is there? Well to put it plainly, there is always and will always be elsewhere. It is this manipulation of human desire by platonic idealism that establishes its immense power base in human affairs. It is in the stranded place, disconnected from life in creation and unable to attain to the ideals that are continually dangled before them, that people become ripe to be ruled and controlled.

Idealism takes a hold of our desire for good, for more of life, for the fullness and attaches it to a never-never land with promises and programming that not many are able to resist. Rather than going into the relational present, we are fixed to a dislocated ideal that does not exist. It is because we are not able to properly engage the present that the fruit God intends us to bear throughout the seasons of life is greatly diminished.

This thinking runs deeply in Western thinking. The church was one of the major carriers of the platonic virus into European history. As such, it is profoundly influenced by idealism – the present kind (the ideal in the thing) and the future kind (the ideal attached to the next life). The market economy has triumphed over most modern minds via the use of present-life idealism. The church used to have a stronger stake in human affairs. This was because it had the patent on how to get to the next life. However, it now finds itself in a media-programmed consumer society unable to be heard because it held out future idealism as the way to get there. It has been tricked into dislodging itself and its people from present life in the spheres of creation and, as such, has little or no meaning or attraction to the many who want to live the life before them.

A church focused on a heaven that exists in a trans-cendent realm outside of life, a church mostly concerned (as many non-Christians perceive) with morality, singing and dying, is not a good bet for those unable to see any substance in what it has on offer. To dislodge from creation is to dislodge from meaning and inheritance. Being bound by thinking that does not permit a full engagement of creation ties you into a very narrow plane of existence.

Within our ever-diminishing circle we are kept, looking and longing for heaven that has little to do with life and work in the spheres of creation. Is it any wonder so little light, salt and leaven make it into the earth underneath our church buildings? Let's now track the journey the platonic stronghold takes in its conquest of the church.

Chapter 5

The Journey from Idea, to Ideal, to Ideology

Time and time again there is a platonic script played out in human affairs. It happens in a local club and it happens in entire nations, its duration is a few years or it lasts for centuries. You have no doubt found yourself either a spectator or a participant in such a play. As an example, I cite one person's account of her experience in the house church movement. 'We once had a group of friends; we worshipped and prayed and witnessed and, basically, lived. It was good. It was so good that we decided to form house churches to best formalise and direct the process. That was ten years ago now. Most of my friends are too busy now – along with myself – running these house churches to get together much anymore. I once had a group of friends.' You will, no doubt, be able to recognise this well-known trend in human affairs. Something that starts out in a relational way takes on a more organised form and over time the organisation becomes more important or real than the very people it was supposedly set up to serve. I believe it is the DNA code laid down by Plato that is determining the course of development here. How does it happen?

The plot can be best understood by looking at the way it unfolds in a three-part play or process. Part one is the idea, part two is the ideal and part three, which is the climax, is the ideology. We will track the rule of ideology in a later chapter; here we look specifically at Plato's use of the idea and the ideal.

An idea can of course be a very good thing. People can come around an idea and work together to see good things arise. The platonic agenda's initial move to take this process off course comes with a subtle shift in emphasis. In line with the platonic worldview, people are made to think that the idea (desire to do a particular thing) actually has a special kind of separate existence. Rather than being understood as a shared relational reality existing between them as people, it is deemed to be something that is 'other' to them. When this happens the idea dislodges from relational reality and, as it were, takes on a distinct or separate life of its own. As the idea takes up the central position over the process the people are progressively moved to the perimeter. Relationships that once shared the good desire between them are now lined up around the 'separate' idea.

Once the idea is dominant the group begins to push it towards what they believe to be its realisation. The idea, with people in tow, is now on the move towards its elusive arrival point. It is at this stage of the platonic play that the idea becomes an ideal. Now most things the group does are measured against the idea. In effect, the idea is beginning to take charge. It now has its own manifest destiny and, if it has not done so already, will soon need to be housed in a company, an institution or a ministry. This promotion from idea to ideal will, of necessity, call for a leader or leaders to oversee the process the idea has put in motion. They will be indispensable to the proper running of the 'idea-housing' vessels. It won't be long before the temptation to become a fully-fledged ideology will come knocking with a deal that will be very hard to resist. When we deem an idea to have a separate existence from the people who share it, when we place it as central and then allow it to regulate our behaviour, we move from platonic idea to platonic ideal and commence the journey towards platonic ideology.

You might be thinking at this point that the above is exaggerating the case. 'Isn't it a good thing to have a shared idea and move around it to achieve something together, incorporating appropriate structures and accountability considerations along the way?' The answer to that is a definite yes. The platonic trick comes in when we begin to think that the idea is something distinct, existing apart from the group. The progression seen in the House Church movement is an example of this. The idea was good – in that to meet in small groups and to encourage initiatives from those groups is a good desire. The shift came in when the 'cell' idea became predominant, when 'it' became the main thing that defined and directed the many good things that were happening and were to happen in that group. When this happened the idea of a cell began to exist as something distinct from the people who actually made up the cell. It took charge, via its leaders, and the people began to follow it towards its event horizon.

The following are quotes from two newsletters/magazines. The first is from an article on cells written for an Evangelical church. It reads:

> It is the responsibility of the church leadership to equip the saints for the work of ministry. We believe that the Cell Group Church approach will most adequately accomplish this goal.
>
> It is the responsibility of every believer to be fruitful in order to multiply the kingdom. We believe that the Cell Group Church approach will most adequately accomplish this goal.
>
> It is the responsibility of every believer to grow and mature in his faith. We believe that the Cell Group Church approach will most adequately accomplish this goal.
>
> There are two things in store for the church in the future: Harvest and Hospitality. We believe that the Cell Group

Church approach will most adequately accomplish this goal.

The Cell Group Church approach is a well-designed plan to enable every believer to be ministered to – to grow and to be prepared to step out in ministry to others.

The second is from a lady in response to attending a conference on the cell method of church. She wrote: 'There is a way forward and CELL IS IT!'

Working hard for work

In response to this you might continue and say, 'I can understand how this might apply to ideas relating to developing a culture, but surely when it comes to things like a product or service, these must have a distinct reality?' In answer I would say that yes, a product, of course, exists as something physically separate to the people who work together to produce and sell it. As such it could be considered as having an existence of its own. That being said, God created the things of earth to be in union with humanity. They are in effect extensions of the image-bearer's life and stewardship. It's like the goods and services we create and consume, they carry and express their maker's attributes, as it were. The nature of the things our work produces is very much an extension of the nature of our humanity.

A small business will express the soul of the individual who runs it. A large corporation will express the collective soul of the founders and the corporate memory inherent to the culture in which it functions. When we treat the product, service or work as 'other' to the people who make or produce it, then we begin to serve the thing itself, rather than serve each other. That is, elemental things that were given for our good become the things that rule us. It is interesting that we do not approach the customer this way, in that we consider the product as one with the aspirations and needs of the purchaser. We inherently know that the more that the product is identified with the person the closer we are to creation reality. We tend however to forget this when it comes to the other side of the sale. All in all, when we remove the idea of work from relational reality by thinking that it is something distinct from us, if we 'idealise' it as being all about the product we produce (or as something measured mostly by the money we make from it), then we fall into the platonic trap. Paul, the apostle, calls this coming under the rule of the elemental things of the world (Gal. 4:3, 9). Our work was never intended by God to define us. We were created to define work, to express ourselves and engage relationships through it.

Imagine a business person who worked hard and long in a company that he jointly owned with several other stake-holders. Over many years he accumulated a good deal of wealth. Once he had amassed enough, he felt that it was time to give something to those who were in need. So, he set up a charity and began to distribute funds. It sounds good and is. However, the fellow was approached during the period of his life that he was accumulating money and was challenged to release more of the good, more of the financial resource along the way; giving his workers more pay and better conditions, his clients more value, his environment more respect and his society more benefit. His response was that he was not working for any of these (excluding perhaps the clients); he was working for himself and his shareholders. He was working to maximise his and their return. The result of this was more money for the company, but less overall good in his own life and the lives of others.

In his work the goal, the distinct idea to make money, was dominant, overriding all other concerns and options that might have been pursued along the way for the good.

The dominant idea had become the ideal and robbed this man and his society of much good. I am not saying that we should not have goals and financial objectives for the work we do. I am saying that if the goal becomes the master then every person involved, inside the company and outside, will be the poorer for it. Idealism does not release prosperity; it ultimately works to strangle the creation purpose.

Cultured ideals

As well as ideas that pertain to tangible products there are also ideas that combine to form our broader relational, social or cultural way of life. It is this latter category of ideas that are of greater interest in relation to the present discussion regarding our culture of church. Again, this progression is seen in the Cell Church example. The idea moves to the centre and front and begins to move the people towards its realisation, the result being that over time people begin to work more for the ideal (and the institution that houses that ideal) than the idea working between and for them. The opportunities for dysfunction are perhaps greater here, because when you do not have a definable product or service, when you are endeavouring to develop a broader culture, then the aims and visions are nowhere near as definable. This means that the arrival point, the ideal outcome, the great goal is more easily shrouded in mystery. As such reality checks, like those that regularly come to those in business selling real goods and services, do not as often visit the church.

My contention again is that, rather than bringing the people involved into creation engagement and the fruit thereof, this 'ideal centred' way of life and work ultimately brings them into bondage to the very things that are meant to serve them. Our works/initiatives and the cultures from which they arise are meant to be our servant. The enemy has taken them and made them our master. History bears out this fact time and time again. Leaders will not always consciously seek to bring people under the rule of the ideal, but repeatedly it happens. People find themselves living to serve an institution that has taken on a life of its own, a life made larger than the people who initially came together to accomplish the task at hand.

One of the reasons why idealism has such a capacity to deceive is because the way of life and work it imposes seems to deliver stronger initial dividends than other alternatives. It follows that when ideas for product or ideas for broader culture are pushed to the centre of the process the projected dividends will often come on line more quickly than otherwise might have been the case. This happens because the work appears to be more simplified. If the ideal rules it is easier for the boss to run its flag up the central pole and get people to salute and obey. Also the idealism in people's way of thinking, one that craves for a golden future via money and markets, will also respond to this way of work more readily. However, as strong as this tower of Babel might appear when first erected on the business or culture plain, the confusion of language and the dislocation of the human heart it brings will, over time, ensure that entropy will be the only winner.

Down the track more and more people will begin to wake up and realise that their work outcomes are diminishing. They realise that the more they work the less it seems to work. They see the initial creativity that got the company or the move happening being crushed. Many people no longer feel valued; rather they feel used. It is at this time that the organisation or ministry, in response to the dismay and withdrawal of the human spirit, will become even more brittle and dysfunctional. The difficulty here is that by this time so much resource and emotion have been invested in the construct housing the ideal that it is too costly, emotionally and financially, to take it out of the way. Most people dare not forsake it. When it does go into a tailspin, such that it has to be rescued, then a new boss with a new broom will come in and sweep the place clean of old leaders and old visions. He will replace these with new leaders and new visions. He will swap the old status quo for a new one. Platonic idealism will always find a way to rule, no matter how many bosses or trends come and go. That is why it must die to us and we must die to it.

Estimated time of non-arrival

The sad thing is that because the ideal does not exist, even when people think they have arrived at it, there will be no real inheritance there for them. The leader, under the influence of the platonic agenda, who finally arrives in his ideal position where 10,000 follow and many ministries are multiplied, will find the anticipated sense of completion sorely lacking. The millionaire who went for that goal in line with platonic idealism finds no fruit and no lasting satisfaction attached to the money he has made. The so-called ideal job is landed and, after a few weeks or months, the same dissatisfaction starts to eat away at you again. The reason being that the ideal is always elsewhere.

A friend went to a conference on work. When he got there he found out that it was actually a conference on unemployment. I suppose that to advertise that would not have inspired as many to come, but that's another story. During the three days of the conference, he met up with a fellow whose passion was for social justice. This was the 'thing' that drove this person to no doubt do many good and noble works. In the course of the conversation the 'social justice' fellow said the following: 'I know that I am treating most of the people who work with me unjustly in terms of pay and conditions. But when we have justice for all, they too will reap the benefits of the improved quality of life that will be there for all.' Here the idea of social justice has taken on a life of its own, distinct from the people who are engaged together in the good desire that this idea expresses. For this fellow the ideal of social justice had become more important, or more real, than the reality or experience of social justice in the relational present. The trouble is that, should social justice arise on a larger scale and hit the fellow in the face, he would not be able to recognise it. He would go on pushing the realisation of his idealised version of social justice into the future. The reason for this being that the ideal he is moving towards does not and will never exist in this finite creation. What does exist all around this fellow is great good in relationship between people. From this good and relational reality so much is there to be released to fill the creation to fullness.

In case some of this chapter got away on you, I include here a brief four-sentence summary:

- The platonic worldview programmes us to believe that ideas are more real than relationships.

- Under its influence we tend to dislodge what should be shared ideas between us and allow them to take up a central position around which we are then arranged.

- Once the idea takes on a separate life of its own and begins to head off, with people following, to its supposed future realisation it becomes an ideal.

- It is given an existence of its own and as such is able to dominate people's lives in a way that God never intended.

The divisive and disabling power of the platonic agenda is now appearing on every side. The church that runs predominately on a platonic operating system is in trouble. Take for instance the last sermon you heard. You remember it don't you? What about the vision statement of your church? Do you still need to be reminded of it? What about those Christians who were full of passion, the ones who were in fellowship here four years ago? Where are most of them now? Remember the ministry trend, the one before last, the one that was going to fill the church by bringing the world through the doors? (No, not that one, the one after that.) Here I am signalling a move further into the contradictions and dysfunctions of our local church culture. Let's look at what this platonic agenda looks like on the troubled surface of local church life.

Life Inside
a House Divided

Chapter 6

The Church (Dis)Engages Creation

God had a divine and eternal idea; it was named church. Platonic philosophy took hold of it and turned it into an ideal. So many things simply don't work out for the current culture and institution of church because of it. As we shall see further down the track, this was the intention from the very start. The ultimate author of this divided worldview never intended that it serve the church. Rather the enemy of our souls designed it to bring us under the control of elemental things and keep from our inheritance in creation. How then is this platonic agenda played out in the local church construct?

Pastor Tim, with every good intention and in line with the theology of church he was taught in college, set up a distinct ecclesiastic domain. He drew a line around the set of activities he managed and called the things he and others did in and from that place 'church'. We looked in the last chapter at the way in which a shared idea takes on a distinct life of its own at the centre of a group and then begins to move them towards its ideal realisation. This is what has happened with the divine idea named church. The church was meant to be a body of people in relationship in Christ growing up through the spheres of creation towards fullness. However, if you ask almost any Christian today which church they belong to, they will tell you that they go to the church of elsewhere, i.e. their church is a distinct social organisation that meets at a certain time, in this place and is led by this person. Even though this is patently not scriptural, it is so much of a given that hardly anyone resists this description anymore. We have taken what was meant to express our relationship together and made it a separate entity on the landscape. By doing so we have, as mentioned, taken a powerful and divine idea and made it an ideal. As soon as we embark on a journey towards platonic idealism we begin to misuse the creation reality. The consequences of this are many and they are not good.

The most obvious problem we come up against relates to the way in which the local church keeps trying extremely hard to be what it is not. Under the present platonic set-up leaders read what the Word says about the church as fullness and apply it for the most part to the set of activities that make up their local church organisation. These truths do in part refer to the gatherings of his body, the church. I am not denying that. The problem is that pastors deem the local church to be the primary dissemination and realisation point for these truths. When they read that Jesus will build his church, they think that it was primarily their local church he had in mind. Christians read the book of Ephesians and then set out to make their local church do things like occupy the heavens, shine light into the darkness of the world system, engage in spiritual warfare in the heavens, equip the saints for works of ministry in creation, bring the church in the city into unity and so on. The fact is that these things cannot be achieved in and from a local church, no matter how large one gets or how many congregations might come to meet in one place at one time. These things can only fully arise through the life and work of the church as fullness. This strategic mismatch ultimately consigns the local church (and its people) to a perpetual and futile attempt to fill up and fill out that which it cannot.

We are left with an immense vacuum in our Christian experience because we no longer have the created order in our sights. The creation was given to us by God to be, as it were, our centre of gravity. Its cry and the inheritance it holds within are the sound and substance that define who we are as sons and daughters of God. We are left with a deeply flawed version of reality because we do not have a creation theology, one that enables us to see and engage the attributes, nature and power of God in, through and over all things. Once the creation is removed we are left with a vacuum, one that draws in all kinds of things to fill the space abhorred. In our attempt to fill up and fill out the immense meaning space left because we took creation out of the mix, we have to invest enormous meaning in the things that make for our church experience (e.g. preaching, creeds, songs, seats, leaders and buildings) and they all become exaggerated way beyond that which God intended. This causes these things and the people that have to deliver on them to come under tremendous strain. They are employed to establish an alternative to creation reality. In this platonic process they become idealised – fixed, separate and other to the saints' life and work in creation.

The three main what might be called 'authority elements' in Christian and church life are the person of the Holy Spirit, the Word and the moral law of God. The preaching, preachers, creeds, worship songs and services all ultimately gain their meaning, their right to exist and function, from these three expressions of God. Let's see how the local church makes use of these to take us away from creation towards what is perceived to be the ideal transcendent realm. The more we fathom this process the easier it will be to understand how the above-mentioned things (preaching, worship, meetings), which express

Spirit, Word and Law are made to function in line with the same agenda.

Church leaders do not do the things I am about to describe with evil intent. Most pastors believe, in accordance with their doctrine of church and creation, that God's people are meant to ultimately be on the move towards a transcendent realm removed from creation. They believe it's their job to take the people on a journey; one marked out by spiritual, moral and truth encounters, away from the present life. They tend to train the saints to engage with a very limited band of life, to involve themselves mostly with only those elements that equate directly with the transcendent (moral, truth) realm; a realm that contains the full and final arrival point for their Christian life. The strange thing is that as ministers teach these things, many believe that they are equipping people for life. To a degree they are, in that any truth taught will make a difference to those who respond. However, the leaven of Plato, the influence that takes the focus ultimately away from this life and puts it in transcendence in the next, works its way through almost every presentation and teaching from the pulpit. This leaven works to tip the balance towards transcendence and away from the saints' present life on earth. The leader's worldview and training have caused them, for the most part, to think that this is the way God would have them take. Let's map in more detail now the course that this journey away from life takes.

Big three in little church

The first step in the platonic ploy is to attach these three authority elements – Spirit, Word and Law – to the local church domain. Taking the name church and fixing it to the buildings, meetings and leaders of the ecclesiastic construct do this. With that done the saints' life and work in creation are effectively moved to the background and the local church's agenda is, by default, elevated to primary player. As such, it commands centre stage and, without any other contenders in view, is deemed to be the main focus of attention for Spirit, World and Law. Whether the church stream has an emphasis on the truth realm or the spiritual realm (both will make use of the moral), the same outcome is in view. As mentioned, this church domain is not heading ultimately in the direction of creation. It is on the move, in line with the platonic vision, to the transcendent and spiritual realm. It is not going in, through, over and up into the heavens above the earth, rather, it is detaching from earth in order to attach to a heaven dislocated from the present age.

Thus, rather than Spirit, Word and Law having to do with the saints' life and work in creation, they have most to do with the church and its mission. This mission, as mentioned, heads into the world a little way but then turns the corner back into a local church on the move towards the transcendent. This orientation means that the activity and ultimate purpose of Spirit, Word and Law are located in, and attached to, the transcendent, rather than the created realm. They become fixed reference and arrival points outside of life. They are mediators between the natural and spiritual realms. They are the door between the temporal and eternal realms. They no longer stand with the saints right through their experience of creation, drawing them up and into the fullness of the third heaven. They now have most to do with the saints' spiritual, moral and truth life – a life mostly identified with their church life and the next life. Ultimately this means that church leaders, preachers, songs and sanctuaries become the focus for Christian life. In this way the platonic course is set, the centre of gravity is fixed. Now very few saints will be able to escape the gravitational pull of the church star. They will remain in orbit around Spirit, Word and Law fixed to a local church construct ever on the way to elsewhere.

It might appear that these three, Spirit, Word and Law, should be authoritive and determinant of all that is said and done in the local church culture. I am in no way denying the authority these have in creation, but I do believe that our platonic orientation has caused us to misuse and mistake the nature of that authority. For a treatment of this matter you might read Chapter 8 of *The Church Beyond the Congregation* – a chapter dealing with creation. Suffice to say here that the authority of these divine expressions of God is without question. However, the nature and purpose of this authority is woven into the creation purpose and the call of God on the life of the image bearer. What this means is that, even though these have the capacity to take initiative, their main role and expression is one of a servant. Their authority is an authority to serve the image bearer so that he or she can move into creation to uncover the inheritance. Like the Father from whom they emanate, these do come with initial strength; it is, however, a strength that gives way (or weaves in) over time to see the sons and daughters emerge into their own in life and work in creation. Then from time to time, as in the Garden, these come and take initiative or enact judgement. Colossians 1:9, 10, which speaks of our good work, and 2 Thessalonians 1:11, 12, which speaks of our good desire in the divine plan indicate this interaction between the divine person and the image bearer. Also, the initial stage of the three phases of the divine strategy has more marked divine initiative and action than the two that follow. A misunderstanding of this creation-oriented strategy causes us to think that the first phase is the only one. Finally, a reading of the Old Testament, with its more direct command and specific prophetic thrust (Law), can again cause us to think that direct, regular commands and initiatives coming from God are the main, or central, way of the divine plan. However, the coming of Christ, bringing the creation purpose back on line (Grace), brought with it a more relational or interactive way of communing with God.

When Spirit, Word and Law are no longer seen as gifts of God to bring us into life in creation, they no longer function the way that God intended. Our response to them is not what it should be. They (via the church agenda) become the focus, the initiators, the enactors, the key to the process because they are fixed mediators of the transcendent realm. The divine plan is no longer about the image bearer in creation. It is now about the Spirit, Word and Law in and from the church construct. This set-up means that our response to them becomes more and more static or fixed. We increasingly give cognitive assent to fixed information about God from the pulpit. We give passive response to the next round of moral correction from the Word. We wait for the next move of the Holy Spirit, our main job being to attract his presence and not get in the way when he decides to come in power. We work on getting enough faith to make us worthy to draw down our healing from the transcendent realm. There is simply not much we can do with things that are authoritative, fixed, central and designed to take us away from our present life in creation.

When good things are attached to a point and place outside of creation, they become like any other ideal thing. They are no longer an expression of our lives, woven into the fabric of our humanity. They are 'other' and have to do with a life that remains ever 'other' to us. Rather than initiating a process that equips and empowers the sons and daughters for their life in creation, these have now become the focal point around which church/Christian life are kept in suspended animation. We spend our lives orbiting around them by orbiting around the people and places that we think define and possess them. It is in this way that the platonic agenda ultimately works to render the local church expression an unworkable enterprise. The church operating within a boundary as a small and distinct authority domain, heading away from creation towards the transcendent/spiritual realm, with idealism dominating its system, does not and cannot work the way God intended it to.

Waiting for eternity

I spoke with a lady who held quite a high position in a transnational corporation, asking her what she thought would turn her workplace around for God. Her response was fairly common for someone in her particular tradition. She said that it is only as we set a platform for worship, via our holiness and devotion to purity, prayer and praise that the manifest presence of God would come into the world. When this happens supernatural displays of power and healing would become a commonplace occurrence in response to the prayers of Christians. Then the world would be convinced of the reality of the Jesus we preach and people would flood into the church. The challenge for this lady is that she had spent the last fifteen to twenty years of her life waiting for that event to occur. Meanwhile all of life, work and creation were and are before her. She was of course doing much good, taking opportunity as it arose. However, imagine how much more could arise if she knew that the work before her was the beating heart of the divine purpose? Will she spend another fifteen years waiting for reality to come from the realm that her church and its ministries have special access to, or will she draw up the well of good and Spirit-filled desire within and be the church as fullness in the spheres of creation she daily engages? This is far from an academic question. It is a matter of one person's entire life.

Far too many lives have gone into a holding pattern, waiting for the Holy Spirit to come and accomplish the divine purpose. When in his mercy God does move in a season of refreshing or even revival, immediately the church culture grasps onto the move for dear life, attaches it to its local church programme and tries to ride it towards what it sees as the finale of God's purposes for the ages. In a few years the water runs out and the fires burn low. When this happens, rather than rethinking their strategy and structure, church leaders and their followers again return to another build-up phase. They return to more of the Word, more holiness, more giving, more worship, more hoping that God will turn up and do what we as saints have been trained and taught not to do. In this holding pattern the very things given by God to empower us, now dislodged from their creation purpose and attached to the agenda of the local church, progressively lose their identity and power in the life of the image bearer. The platonic agenda works to ensure that the people of God are made passive and rendered dependent on the very things that were given to empower them for life. The ramifications of this outcome are many and varied. It impacts adversely on saints, creation, angels and the gathering. Let's now look at the kind of church construct that the divided life gives rise to.

Chapter 7

The Collapsing House

Viewed objectively, as much as one can accomplish such a feat, the local church in one instance appears to be a very normal thing and then in another a rather strange arrangement. The strangeness comes in whenever you stop to consider what Jesus Christ came to accomplish on earth and then compare that culture of the local church against the intensity and depth of that mission. In the incarnation we are presented with God coming as man to save, redeem and restore the entire created order through the life and work of the body of Christ. This body is now, for the most part, associated with buildings and endless meetings. Most of the work saints engage in as the church revolves around keeping these buildings and the meetings therein happening. When compared to the creation-encompassing purpose for the church, the local church as a vehicle to match or express that divine strategy is really quite a let-down.

If you have a church of a hundred adults then at best you might have three 'out there to the community' ministries and perhaps one or two persons you are supporting in part in another country. That is generally how much most local churches can cope with. From there, as mentioned, most of the rest of the energy goes into keeping the buildings and the meetings ticking along. Larger churches might appear to have more ministries and thus more impact, but pro rata the larger the numbers the less proportionate are the numbers of ministries these churches produce. That is, they appear to do more, but in effect do less. Again most of the energies of the people involved in these congregations are taken up running the internal programme for the Christians that come.

When compared to the creation-encompassing purpose in the incarnation, the local church as a vehicle to match or express that divine initiative is really a no-show. Its ability to make headway in our present society is trifling, because it continues to define itself as an ecclesiastic unit on some street corner. For the local church to pretend to be the church as fullness flies in the face of commonsense and the divine purpose. However, year in and year out it keeps trying. If the church as construct were the only option we had, then we would have to make the best of it. However, there is an alternative. It is the church as fullness. The problem is that for all kinds of theological and vested reasons the church local cannot or will not loosen its grip on the kingdom process.

The pastor's training has, as mentioned, led him to believe that the church gathered is the church prime and proper. The saints, in line with this doctrine, are taught to think that the church can only properly be church if it gathers under the wing of its leaders in the sanctuary. This thinking also extends to the house church movement. One wonders where on earth the church goes when it is not meeting? Some have a theology that enables them to speak of the church gathered and the church scattered. Others, in line with the charismatic development in ecclesiology, distinguish between the church in the meeting and the kingdom out there in society. A more modern version of this teaching speaks of the kings who rule in business and the priests who run the church. The motifs used here might have some benefit as an illustration, in that they have helped to establish a better relationship between the household and the fullness. However they still leave the church gathered as central and the church as fullness, by definition, secondary and subservient. They still leave us with the old dualism that sees the local church occupying the sacred and the kingdom happening in the secular. If we are to overcome and be the fullness of him who fills all, we need a seamless way of being church in all areas of life. Any, and all, divides must be closed and one body must be allowed to emerge in answer to creation's cry.

The local church, considering itself to be the primary expression of the church on earth, has in effect set up shop in what it thinks is its own sphere of creation – a sphere that was never created by God.

> We have taken the organisational dimension of life and placed it over us. We named it an organisation and we brought it to life. We stamped a vision statement on it, placed it in a legal construct, gave it a brochure and a building and sent a cash flow through it. The outcome is that most leaders and saints now live to serve it.
>
> James Thwaites, *The Church Beyond the Congregation*, p. 185

Essentially, the local church as something separate to the saints' lives is not a creation reality. Inside its bounded circle the local church has drawn almost all of the resources, truths and authority that belong to the church as fullness. For this and other reasons I believe that the church as separate construct is not a valid expression of the kingdom purpose.

Yes, the gathering of God's sons and daughters, the agreement between saints, the servant authority given to elders, the good desire of people, the input of ministry gifts and the shared culture these create are all very real and good. However, I believe that the authority construct in which all these good and divine things are presently defined and confined is invalid. When we look at a local church in operation we do see many good things happening. However, the platonic leaven works from the centre to permeate the entire church lump, effectively working against the very good that centre was initially set up to accomplish. This construct forms into and/or joins with what Tom Marshall called a corporate entity or spirit, one whose power (both fallen angelic and human) is very strong and is the cause of much dysfunction.

We will look in more detail at the composite make up of this corporate entity in a later chapter. Suffice to say here that it is important that we understand the different elements, good or otherwise, that make for such an entity. Again, the God-given and good elements found in the church as construct are not our problem. Rather, our difficulty lies in the way in which these are always collapsing into a construct that forms a corporate spirit or entity over people and process. It is as we discern what the creation goods are and who the strong man holding them is that the binding of him and the loosing of them can begin (cf. Mk. 3:27; Mt. 18). Again, we will come back to this matter further on. For the present it is sufficient to say that the church as construct is a power structure that must go into death. It is only through this dying process that the people and the good within it will be able to emerge into the new creation expression of Christ's body, the church. Let's look inside the church as construct and endeavour to fathom more of the how and why of its dysfunction.

View from the pulpit

When pastors look out on Sunday morning to make that third and final sermon point, what kind of entity do they see themselves managing? What is it about the organisation before them that renders it an unworkable enterprise? What makes it a hothouse in which so many flowers wilt? We won't have time to cover every single aspect of the answer to these questions because (i) I am unaware of many of them at the moment and (ii) there is so much complexity and interaction in any relationship that you could not hope to express it in a few pages. There must be a third point to make this paragraph valid, but I cannot think of it now. Let's look at some of the problems afoot in the church house.

The people of God are presently kept inside what might be called a collapsing house. What do I mean by this? The elders, the ministry gifts, the people and the works of ministry all presently operate for the most part in and from little organisational units. In contrast to this, the Scriptures speak of the church as the body of Christ, his people living and working throughout a city or a region – the church at Ephesus, the church at Jerusalem and so on. The concept of distinct legal entities on the corner of High and Main Street managed by a pastor was not something that the early saints would have understood. They did not see different gatherings as distinct churches, but instead saw them as simply expressions of the church they were.

Elders were given authority to safeguard and oversee the health of the environment in which the church in the city existed. Their work was to ensure that there was food, nurture and safety for the saints to enable them to grow up in all things. This did involve times of discipline and direction as the need arose. This city-wide dispersion of elders contrasts with the present layout where several elders manage and direct each congregation. The early church elders did not order the works of ministry of the saints or manage the weekly programme of Christian activities for the church. They understood the difference between guarding a space for its well-being and managing it by taking charge of the people and process. These elders were never in charge of the church in the city, no one was in charge of it except Jesus Christ.

Ministry gifts of Christ – pastors, teachers, apostles, evangelists and prophets – also served the church throughout the city. Of course a good deal of their time would have been spent with saints as they gathered, but again they did not see this expression of church as being the centre of the kingdom process. As such their equipping of saints for works of service was for all of life, rather than primarily an equipping for local church life. Certainly one can be an elder and a ministry gift, but to confuse the two (particularly when you think that elders are in charge of the church) is a mistake. Paul did work with a specific team of people to accomplish the mission God had given him. However, our modern day pastors/elders, thinking they are taking their cue from the apostle, have in effect turned their congregations into their very own ministry team.

The current church culture has fused elder and ministry gift into the office of managing pastor and created a hybrid that holds far too much power over far too small a space. What was meant to be a city-embracing body of people is collapsing into a confined space bounded by a building and defined by a meeting. It's like having the house of parliament on the third floor, the administrative services on the second and the children turned into workers on the ground, pressed in to serve the agenda of the floors above. Any other household in your street that did the same would be liable to attract the attention of child welfare. This dysfunction in our way of being church ultimately creates dysfunction in our pastors and in those who follow them. Inside this collapsing house our pastors and their people are working very hard and very long to try and realise the unworkable. Let's see how this is accomplished.

Homogenised saints

The first and perhaps the most telling outcome of this line of church sight is that the saints' life and work in creation are out of focus to church leaders. The meeting in the building naturally captures the pastor's perpetual attention because it is considered to be the key to the kingdom process. This means the pastor works primarily to build the people of God for church life. In this their 'out there' life and work do have a part to play, and they will refer to it and teach about it from time to time. However, all of the main roads come from and return to the local church building.

As a consequence, the pastor can end up relating to people more as part of a homogenous entity called church than as individuals. The people form (in the pastor's mind) into a kind of collective mass. The pastor's calling is to motivate, disciple and mobilise this block of saints to accomplish the church mandate. To assist in the management of this process people are broken down for simplicity's sake into leaders, loyal regulars, fringe dwellers, out of fellowship, backslidden and then, of course, beyond the church there are the lost. Rather than seeing the church as fullness and relating to the diversity of people's life, initiatives and work, the pastor simplifies the church process and the church people to fit them into his organisational grid. This produces a church culture that is simple, uniform, narrow and often quite bland. It also means that the pastor will expend much of his energy over the years just trying to get people into what he thinks is the church centre.

It hardly needs to be said, but such an approach impacts strongly on the way in which the saints grow and engage life in God. As mentioned, pastors encourage their people to do other things in life beside church. But these 'other things' are still deemed to sit outside the church borders. They happen away from the middle ground marked out by the pastor as sacred and special. As such they are not the pastor's main concern and hence are not provisioned or named like the church proper. Is it any wonder that so many personal ministry initiatives do not prevail against the gates of hell? Indeed, the fact that many of them falter is used to shore up the thinking that says the church local must be the only proper version of church.

A pastor I spoke with expressed the concern that if we pursued the concept of church in all of life, then people would do their own thing, there would come a scattering and unity would be lost. My response to him was that we need to develop new understandings and practice for those called as ministry gifts. We need to encourage elders to establish an 'out there' culture to emerge, one in which the saints can grow, relate together and make their impact. It was no use saying it won't work if ministry gifts, by their lack of involvement and input, ensure that it does not. This is like giving your son a dollar and telling him to start a business and then chiding him when it failed due to lack of finances. The second thing, in response to his question, was a question to him on my part. I asked, 'When the hundred or so people who come to church on Sunday sit before you in chairs, do you really think that they are in unity?' These people, I said, are thinking a hundred different things, desiring this and wanting that, going after that goal and recovering from their last attempt at another. In all, these folk, in most areas of their life, are a thousand miles away from real church unity.

By defining unity so narrowly we think we have achieved it because people are regular in attendance, give assent to the pastor's teaching and in part respond and give to the vision of their leaders. This is not the unity that Jesus prayed for. This is not the kind of unity that will see the world sit up and take notice. The context in which Paul speaks of the unity of the body is the creation. The unity of the saints is affected as they do the works of service together in creation. Paul says that we are joined together as one body 'by that which every joint supplies' (Eph. 4:16). The supply relates to the work and the work is in creation. Judged in this light the body of Christ has very little unity indeed. We are not one in the work. We are not one in creation. Instead we are being substantially kept in con-gregations away from our inheritance and fellowship together in creation. Only when ministry gifts and elders release and equip the saints to live, work and gather in the many and diverse places of life will we know the unity that makes for the many-faceted kingdom life designed by our creator God.

Our bounded and intense culture ensures that much more planning, talking and meeting have to be done in the local church than otherwise would be the case. Most pastors are trained to think that their mission is to perfect the church process; thinking that this will have a flow-on effect in the life of the saints and from there into the world. What is of note in this perfecting process is the smallness of many of the things leaders try to perfect. It's amazing to sit with ministers and hear their conversation about church. Much of the talk tends around issues pertaining to the music, sermon, furniture, equipment, the giving, and, of course, the ever-present building or the lack thereof. These are the elements and these are the people that the pastor has to forge into a unified army to take the world. Certainly lots of local churches do great things and I am not decrying the good these accomplish. However, compared to the creation mandate to fill all things church-based ministries, even if they do happen to achieve a measure of success, are still light years away from responding to the extent and depth of the cry. To perfect the imperfectable is a never-ending job that keeps pastors and people employed inside the collapsing house for centuries.

The vision thing

Bringing the local church construct to life as a distinct legal entity means we have to keep moving it about to convince others and ourselves that it's alive. A powerful tool used to accomplish this feat is a thing called 'the vision'. In its best and most functional expression a vision, or mission statement is an attempt to describe in a sentence or two the shared culture and purpose of a group of people. This, of course, serves to establish a stronger sense of belonging and cooperation between people. If the vision thing were only this, there would be no problem. However, as we have seen the platonic agenda has come in, taken a hold of the culture and purpose and has placed them under leaders in a construct. What was meant to be a shared and diverse culture of agreement between saints has now become a uniform construct separate to and over them. What was (perhaps) intended to be a shared statement of belief and intention between people is brought to life and pressed into service as something very different.

The vision thing came out of America, a nation where, as mentioned, idealism and corporate reality rule more than anywhere else on earth. Evangelicals, Pentecostals, charismatics and many older traditional churches generally use some form of it. Pentecostals and charismatics generally use the term vision, whereas more conservative streams use 'mission statement' or, if there is a need for more subtlety, the term 'philosophy of ministry' is used. Any one of these will serve the same basic purpose. They are employed by most ministers to help people understand what the particular church is and what it is going to do. However, once inside the system, the vision thing downloads much more than its résumé declared at the initial interview. This psychological weapon is critical to the platonic game plan. It is able to invest the pastor's middle ground with authority, meaning and definition, bringing the church centre to life like nothing else can. It is essential to have some form of vision thing in place if one is to move the church from the rule of idealism to the rule of ideology.

Pentecostal and charismatic leaders generally get their vision directly from God. Others get theirs from God via the 'consensus of the saints' approach. Whichever way it comes, once in hand the leaders have something that defines the reason for the being and beating heart of their local or cell church. You have no doubt read a few vision statements, or perhaps been involved in developing them. Here are a few I have read.

- Reaping the harvest to feed the nations.

- To know God and make him known.

- A church large enough to help and small enough to care.

- A church for our city and beyond.

- Turning the tide from death to life in Marsden.

- A contemporary church where the anointing on the life of the senior pastor comes to rest on the people.

Vision statements, when examined, are most often couched in ideal form. They are generally constructed by presenting scriptural truths in an ideal and grandiose way. As such, they can never really be fathomed, fixed as they are to some immeasurable and ever-future arrival point. These statements often are more connotation statements than descriptive of any measurable intent, but, as we shall see, that is not a problem. In fact the less these statements mean the more power they can have over the people, the process and ultimately the pastor. Once attached to the centre, the vision is deemed to belong to the church rather than to the people as individuals. This effectively brings the church as construct into a life that is deemed to be more important than that of the people. It appears reasonable to most that something stamped with a divine imprimatur must be real, central and primary and thus worthy of the saints' backing. Once in place the vision effectively takes a special kind of authority over the process and the people. The route the vision takes in gaining this authority is often hard to trace. Let's endeavour to follow the progression as observed in many, if not most, Pentecostal/ charismatic settings.

The leader is given a vision by God for the church. The church comes into being and is seen as doing so in fulfilment of the vision. The pastor has been entrusted with the vision and hence is the main interpreter, minder and implementer of it. People don't directly serve the pastor; instead they are encouraged to serve the vision – a vision that just happens to have come via the pastor. Without him you do not have a vision from God. With him you have a vision and hence a place in the divine plan. The leader is deemed to be a servant of the vision and correspondingly appears to serve the church to ensure the vision's fulfilment. This set-up makes people think that their pastor is not directly taking charge of the church. They think he is simply serving a vision that came from God. As such his control over the people and the process and the name church is less obvious and thus more acceptable.

Even in those settings that occasionally speak of the importance of pursuing one's dreams and desires, the primacy of the church's vision over any other contenders', which are secondary and subservient, ensures that a clear message rings through. Many local churches do incorporate human desire into their programme. However, it is only if these desires or giftings happen to match with a need the church has that they will be commissioned into the service of the church. If they are outside of the vision loop then they are deemed to be important only so far as they might indirectly contribute to the work of the church. I do not believe that we can have two centres of the divine purpose, one the local church and the other the individual heart. Such an arrangement is not spoken of in Scripture. One will take precedence over the other and should there be any contest, we know which one will rule the roost.

So high you can't get over it

The following is an excerpt from an article on unity from a Pentecostal magazine. The heading of the paragraph is 'Hidden or Different Agendas'. Underneath the heading we read:

> Then there are those with a different vision and mindset which is contrary to, or does not quite link up, with the church's corporate vision. At times their vision may not be evil as such, or even totally wrong, yet, because it is at odds with the church's, unity is forfeited. All private visions must be laid down and the church's corporate vision accepted.

One can immediately see why the vision thing is so useful to the platonic agenda. Once in place no one, except the leaders, can easily get at the church's centre. You can't get around the vision because it permeates the entire church process. You can't get to the bottom of it because no one can ultimately fathom it. If you speak against it, as is the case with any ideology, then by definition you must be a heretic and should be disregarded. If you don't understand it then know that your leader, who got it from atop the mount, truly knows and thus duly serves the vision.

The vision thing sends a clear communication to the Christian: it is only if you identify with the church, defined by its vision and its leader, that you can share in the realisation of the ideal that the church is going after. The word used to describe this way of life is vicarious – meaning to live your life through another person or thing. What goes missing in this ecclesiastic interplay is, of course, the life and work of the sons and daughters of God in creation. Church is no longer really about them and their lives. It's about the church construct and its life. It's about the leader's exploits and the church's ministries. It's about the vision thing, the future ideal and the need to commit your life to the church, which alone can take you through to the prize. This enshrines the power of the pastors over the process; enabling the organisation they lead to appear larger and more important than the life of any one, two or more of their church members.

We saw how confusion in our ecclesiology has caused most church leaders to treat their congregations as if it were their own ministry team. They have taken their own personal desire and vision and made them the mandatory desire and vision for the mass of people they think are their church. This is neither scriptural nor appropriate. It's time that we gave ourselves permission to see through the vision thing. We can commend leaders for having a desire from God and can of course choose to work with them in different initiatives they undertake. These initiatives are not, however, the church primary, they are simply a part of the diverse mosaic of work that is done by his body, the church in every sphere of creation. In fact, when it comes to the question of priority, the leader's desire is not on equal footing with that of the saints. Leaders are called to be servants of the saints, equipping them for every good work in creation. As such the saints' works are more important than that of the leaders. I know that most leaders do set out to be servants of the people of God, but is it not strange that they end up with so many people serving them and the institution they created on behalf of those same people?

A pastor got up in a large church I attended recently. He spoke of the incredible things the church had accomplished in the past year – the church plants, the music produced, the crowded conferences, the building extensions and, yes, even some outreach to the disaffected. As the thousand or so people listened, many no doubt felt good about what 'they' as a church were doing. The reality was that not more than 5 per cent of them were directly involved in any of these activities. For the most part these people simply turned up, gave money, worshipped in song and listened to speakers. Their ideal life of kingdom ministry was taken care of by their leaders and their real life of everyday activity remained begging outside the gate.

Vision, vision on the wall

I suppose it's not really all that strange that over time most churchgoers ignore vision statements. What you find is that after a few months or a year the vision that was carried into the sanctuary with much pomp and fanfare, now hangs on the wall neglected by most and understood by few. Leaders, to arrest this entropy, have to continually paint the vision on banners that move in the breeze of the ceiling fans. They have to print them in bold on their church letterhead and parade them at the end-of-year celebration and the start-of-year commitment Sunday. All this to remind people of how much the vision has done for them and what it is they have to keep fighting to give more for. Even when the vision is ignored, or scoffed at by a few heretics, its power remains intact. The reason being that it is deemed to occupy the centre and hold to itself the authority of that centre. Like the traditional churches whose influence over the life of those who never attend is still strong (because these hold the rights and resources of the church inside), the vision does not even have to be powerful to take power away from the saints.

Some might think that this kind of set-up is tailor made for the leader, but over time even they are dislodged and disempowered. Once the vision is attached to the church construct, then all kinds of market and platonic forces come into play to take it further and further away from the leader. Over the years, they can become, like others, the harried servant of the vision. Visions have to keep looking alive and delivering something. They have to keep moving on, producing stuff and meaning much. One visionary leader of a large congregation was heard to say in a moment of doubt that he now realises that over a thousand people are waiting on his next word, needing him to tell them what to do next. This fellow has to keep promising more and doing more to justify his existence as leader and keeper of the flame. He started out using the vision thing married to idealism to build his church and now finds himself living to feed those made dependent on him because of what he has made. He is no longer really a leader; he has become the lackey of platonic idealism.

The simple middle ground we have created and named as church increasingly suffers under the weight of its own self-inflicted glory. Even in so-called successful churches inertia starts to weigh in over time. The larger a thing gets the simpler the definition of the middle has to become and the more the centre has to busily keep it all going. The bigger the church the greater its centre of gravity and hunger for resources. This is a well-known phenomenon in corporations that actually have a distinct product to sell.

To think that the church, an institution that introduced the rule of idealism into the West, will be able to side step such an outcome is to dream.

The church construct set in place by the platonic agenda ensures that the homogenous group on Sunday will take precedence over the individual, the leader will take precedence over the followers, the church vision and ministry will take priority over personal desires and initiatives and the kingdom's life and power will belong to the church as construct and not the church as people. It ensures that most all of the divine resources that should be dispersed throughout creation are captured and tied to church as pillar and support. This ensures that the people of God will never be the church, kept as they are serving leaders, buildings and visions that have taken that name church from them. You can never fully be the church if your church is something and somewhere else. The effect of all of this on the pastor, the preacher and the people is profound. It creates an ecclesiastic merry-go-round spinning its way to nowhere. It's no wonder so many are not purchasing a ticket for the next ride. The pastor as preacher, elder and manager, ever trying to keep the thing spinning, stands in the middle of the ecclesiastic loop. Let's climb up into the pulpit and look out over what has been created by his many words and ministrations inside the collapsing house.

Chapter 8

Plato Among the Preachers

A preacher once delivered an incredible sermon. It was one that shook the church and was spoken about for days afterwards. The title was 'Out of the Cave and into the Harvest'. The cave was the church building and the harvest was the world out there. The words came like a torrent, full of genuine conviction and powerful eloquence. 'We must get out into the streets. We must move out and occupy the city. We must reach out and bring in the lost.' On the river of this thirty-five minute Sunday evening message went. The challenge to this oft repeated topic is that the person who was preaching it spent most of his life in the cave designing programmes for the people who were listening. The affirmation and patterning for life in the cave came from the person who was trying to get all the people out of the cave. Also, the very phrase 'out of the cave' suggested that these people were living in the cave. The truth was that most of their week was spent in their work places and in their homes. That is, they were already out there, but because the church in the mind of this preacher was 'in here', then they as the church could only be the church out there if they got out of the 'in here'. One can begin to see the difficulty that arises for the listeners in relation to this logic. Still, that being said, the sermon was a great one and inspired many for days to come. The problem is that most of the life and work of the saints who really are out there remain, for the most part, invisible to the leaders of this church culture. At last count they were still trying very hard to get everybody out by getting everybody in!

The pulpit and the pastor in charge of it are both the main weapons and major assets of the local church. These, working as one, are the steering wheel that regulates the engine room and together set the course for the church journey. The preacher is called to lead, the saints are meant to follow and between them sits the Bible. What are we to make of this arrangement? Or more so, what has the platonic agenda made of it? Preachers are the main spokesperson for the 'ideal' version of church. They are the main interpreters of the what, who and why of the Spirit, Word and Law. The words they utter week by week are seen to emerge from the divine and transcendent realm, helping to direct most of the traffic from this world to the next. For these, and other reasons, this means that preachers and their pulpits are well placed to express 'presentation symptoms' of that which afflicts the body of Christ.

Some of these 'symptoms' appear directly as a result of the platonic agenda. Others arise from unsound educational practices in the local church. Many, if not most of these practices are also derived from the platonic, but in a secondary rather than a primary way. Of course human choice and dysfunction also works *its* way through the mix as well. I don't want to give the impression that Plato is responsible for everything that happens at church. He, like the devil, is not all-powerful, nor is he all-responsible. So, what is going wrong with preaching? Why is so much Bible teaching producing (as the surveys suggest) so little Bible knowledge? Why is so much education resource not producing saints and congregations able to impact their city? Why has something so powerful become so weak?

Revelation drag

Let's start with an educational issue – the simple problem of too much of a good thing. This arises from the platonic-induced problem associated with the church gathered trying to act like the church as fullness. The preaching event is called on to fill up an immense amount of the space left because of the vacation of the creation from the divine strategy. This means that there is a whole lot more preaching in the church recipe than was ever intended by God. Sunday after Sunday, conference after conference, tape after video after tape, the committed church attendee hears volumes of words coming from the ecclesiastic domain. The problem is that they simply do not have time to put a fraction of what they hear into action before they are ushered in to the next 'crucial' or 'essential' message demanding yet more response. Year in and year out this takes its toll on the Christian's ability to hear and integrate truth into life. They become accustomed to listening and used to the fact that they do not, because they cannot, assimilate what is heard into their understanding or practice.

Saints over time, in a word-flooded environment, reach a place where they have pretty well heard it all. Here the 'nothing new under the sun' clause makes it way into the church contract. Their response to the Word increasingly becomes an evaluation of the preacher rather than an encounter with truth. They increasingly control/regulate the way they permit sermons to influence them. An expertise in sermon tasting comes from building up certain tastes over years of church attendance. This causes a doctrinal block to form in the mind of saints. The result is that most every sermon (and preacher) comes to be evaluated on the extent to which it agrees or disagrees with that disposition. In this way the preaching event becomes more about the sermon's delivery than the saints' life.

The Bible carries within it an educational approach that, for the most part, we overlook in our never-ending stream of words from the pulpit. Most saints are too busy trying to keep up with the information coming from the ideal realm attached to their local church to apply God's truth to their own life and work. Because of this the hunger God intended they have for life in creation is greatly diminished. This produces a corresponding lack of hunger for the bread of life. The result is more fast food outlets being set up with increasing numbers of saints coming to pick at preachers and choose little among the truths on offer at the salad bar.

Sacramental

The next symptom arises more directly from the platonic agenda. What becomes apparent over time is that saints increasingly relate to the preaching event more as a fixed sacrament than as wisdom to be integrated into their lives. Certainly they continue to take knowledge about God from the sermons they hear, but this is overtaken by the more pressing need to be spiritually blessed and assured by the Sunday sermon. Access to the Spirit, Word and the Law is now predominately via the preacher because the focal point for reality has been moved away from ordinary life. This causes the preaching event to take on the role of primary mediator between the natural and spiritual realms. Thus, the preacher and his words of grace, comfort and wisdom in effect become sacramental.

The transition from person as pastor to priest as sacrament is easily made because the leader is the personification (the defining personality) of the church entity and Word of God. If your job is to perpetually appear to identify with the transcendent realm removed from life, then people will begin to use you as a sacrament to get through to that realm. If you represent the ideal realm you will be idealised. Real sacraments like water baptism or the Lord's Table are meant to have a more fixed form, because they speak of past, present and future givens that do not change. This is tremendous when it comes to actual sacraments, but when applied to the living Word it is a tragedy. Those who live by the ideal will often end up dying by it.

Up on the mount, behind the ecclesiastic barrier, preachers become encased in perspex pulpits and the wood of their office, their humanity submerged behind their priestly functions. This humanity is brought out occasionally for careful display to teach a truth or two, or dragged out for a sacrifice if the congregation turns against their leader in seasons that demand a scapegoat. People connect with the office of pastor, but don't seem to connect with the man himself. Those who are in streams where actual priests feature are more accustomed to this. There the man is not meant to get in the way of the sacrament. He, in effect, becomes one with it. In the more contemporary settings many leaders thought that they would be able to side step the priestly robes. However they are finding themselves increasingly living the life of an altar boy.

Some pastors are better able to resist this tug of war. Others, believing their own platonic advertising, actively make use of it to generate a following. Most live in the muddled middle. As the pastor becomes more wrapped up in the ideal, he becomes more fixed as a sacrament and more muffled as a man. Over time, even the so-called radical leader becomes schooled by the congregation's response as to what he should and should not deliver. If he does not supply then they will wander. If he does supply then they will follow, or at least keep turning up on Sunday. It may take years, but our 'radical' leaders will, over time, only sound radical. Their pulpit push to drive the people into the revolution becomes increasingly besieged by spectators waiting for the next ideal sermon point to be scored on their behalf. The more this happens the less the leader is able to move into new territory. If he does move too far he will stretch and break the contract that gives to the people the security and identity they have been programmed to need so much of. So it is that stagnation and unreality becomes the portion for most of our ideal, sacramental and once radical leaders.

I spoke with a Baptist minister and he said that the core of his church consisted of strong believers, totally committed to sound Baptist doctrine. The problem was that he could not do anything with them. 'They nod heartily when I push one of their Baptist buttons and get confused when I say anything new. If I keep going on about new things their perplexity turns to a frown. We're stuck! I'd like to put a (metaphorical) bomb under them so that this church can go somewhere. But I dare not do it.' The need to hear the same things regularly extends also to the more cutting-edge church climate. There the need to be radically challenged to live an extraordinary life is standard preaching fare. Preachers in these settings deliver heart-stopping, big picture, get out of the rut sermons and sure enough people are struck by the force. The problem is that many of the hearers think they are being radical just because they agree with the sermon. Of course some do change in response to the challenging words and in particular newer Christians are often moved. Over time, however, there is only so much 'radical' that one can take before it becomes mundane.

It might appear from verses like the one in 2 Timothy 3:16, which speaks of the Word of God being 'profitable for teaching, reproof, for correction, for training in righteousness', that the Word is in fact meant to fill up lots of space and be central to the entire kingdom process. I want to tread carefully here, but what is of note in regards the Scripture is just how much it does not say about the how, where and what of our lives – it has a lot more to say about the why. To complete the passage quoted from Timothy, these great things from the Word of God are all given to equip the saint for 'every good work' in creation. These works are not described in detail; the reason being that God wants us to discover them ourselves. Jesus spent most of his time sketching the outlines and co-ordinates of the emerging kingdom, teaching the nature of it rather than filling in all the gaps. The great and divine educator knew that there was no use telling all about the kingdom before it emerged in the heart, life and work of the kingdom people. Like Paul, Jesus understood that it would be through the fruit of our good works in creation that our primary experience of life, inheritance and God would arise (Col. 1:10).

The lion and the lamb

Another counter-productive interplay between preacher and listener has to do with the way that saints are kept at a fairly low peg on the moral development scale. This arises because of the continued emphasis on the need for a moral response to the Word that is preached. We are producing Christians who have very strong opinions on just a few subjects, people not able to live with much tension in life because they have not been trained to do so. One might say that we are creating lots of binary saints – people who have a right/wrong or on/off response to most of life's questions.

Do an exercise if you will. I have done it numerous times and find it fascinating. Assess, in the next ten sermons you hear, the number of times you are told things the preacher says you don't know and should know. Count the number of times you are corrected, rebuked or challenged to do more, give more, be more. As noted, the Word of God is profitable for teaching, reproof, correction and training. However the constant flood of information vying for influence tends preachers much more towards reproof and correction than it does teaching and training. Wisdom and reason take a whole lot longer to get across the line, but if the hearer is made to think they are in the wrong and need to get it right, then their response will generally be much more immediate.

The outcome of this is that many Christians believe that their main response to preaching is to understand and obey it. Both of these responses can, of course, be correct. However the result is that saints begin to think that if they are obeying what they have heard from the preacher then they have adequately responded to God himself. The simplicity of most messages and their moral appeal to conscience means the most pressing issues of Christian life tend to revolve around things like 'are you praying enough, are you witnessing enough, are you giving, attending, being honest and loving enough?' The answer to these is in part yes, but in the final analysis is always no.

In this kind of climate many harried listeners become dislodged from the never-ending attempt to arrive at the behavioural ideal portrayed from the pulpit. They give up trying to measure up, feeling that their Christianity has become one long moral exam that they never seem to pass. Many Christians also lose confidence in their ability to understand, discern and take initiative. They don't need to do much 'Christian' thinking because Sunday by Sunday the preacher, the one who knows what is right and what is wrong, in effect does most of it for them. They are not being trained to see deeply into their inheritance in creation.

Their relationship with God and with life therefore tends much more towards the basic and binary, rather than the richness and diversity God desires for them. It's no wonder that many outside of the faith consider Christians to be opinionated and naive in their approach to the real issues of life and obsessed with a narrow band of moral issues.

Another response is observed in people who, when it comes to their everyday life perform like lions, but come Sunday as they enter through the church doors they act like lambs. As they sit in the pews they meekly listen to moral lessons from the life of Jeremiah, or sit quietly while they are challenged again to do something of substance with their faith. In response to this they might experience some religious guilt, learn a moral truth to think over when time permits or take a choice truth or a funny story with them as they head out the door to resume the life of a lion. In religion they are passive and dependent, in work they are active and take initiative like normal people. In all, as sons and daughters of God, they are divided and they are conquered.

Ideally speaking

In the contemporary church culture the leadership thing is, as we know, very much in vogue. To have a dynamic person with a great message and a vision that heads off into a guaranteed future is fundamental to market success. If you don't have these qualifications then you either reinvent yourself, plod along with a smaller number following you, or get out altogether. Many pastors are left with all three of these options, each in conflict with the others and all straining to compete in the one bewildered soul. However, when it comes to Sunday this confused soul is put aside as this person, confident in the message they carry, sure of the direction they must take and positive for reasons they cannot quite articulate, mounts the pulpit to speak again about the mission of the church, the power of the kingdom and the guarantee of a great future.

If you cannot give the saints the reality God has for them in the present age, then you will need to compensate by promising them something else. Now of course heaven awaits us in the age to come, a heaven now existing over the earth. Once, however, heaven is removed from the current equation then a strong platonic lean has to enter in to compensate. Once what is real is taken away from us then what is ideal has to be brought in to fill the void. Idealism's platonic realisation point for its promises is located for the most part in the after life, but, as we have seen, idealism also has a present life version as well. This 'ideal' replacement for reality is housed in the church vessel and is downloaded by the pastor via the ceremony of the pulpit.

The older traditions communicate their idealism via the sacraments and/or the liturgy. The evangelicals emphasise 'truth' or 'creed' as the key to the transcendent. The holiness movement go for purity as the way through to the perfect realm. Enter the Pentecostals and their cousins the charismatics. These go for the encounter event via the means of worship and preaching. Please note that I am not against any or all of these, rather I am drawing reference to the platonic influence that takes a hold of their particular core emphasis and uses it to move the saints away from creation towards the ideal realm. The leaven of the ideal has been there for many centuries in different ways in every denomination. However, it is the contemporary church's exaggeration of the practice that helps to draw out this leaven into the light of day.

To put it simply, for ministers to get ahead these days they have to appear to have something special going for them. Like politicians, but with less funding and power, preachers increasingly have to sell themselves like a product to the 'discerning' church shopper. The market is ever in search of a good service and if the preacher does not deliver then he and his ministry will be consigned to oblivion. Increasingly we are seeing, in particular in more contemporary church settings, a push for this person and their word to function as a kind of intoxicant. The strong pulpit rush of golden promises and great exploits causes the people to feel bonded to greatness for the time these take to travel through their system. And when the blast is over they return to their mundane existence, often none the wiser and still pining for life. No problems here, because this means that they will be back next Sunday wanting more. Our idealised way of preaching ensures that most of the power of the Word is consumed in the event itself. Very little makes it out of the parking lot and into the life and work of the saints. We have made far too many sons and daughters addicted to listening to what is left of a Word ravaged by idealism. The divided world in which preachers are forced to market themselves ensures that most all of the power and people are kept seated and made dependent inside the collapsing house.

Ceremony men

The leaven of platonic idealism works to produce pastors detached from the very thing and the very people they are meant to be leading. It effectively isolates them in ecclesiastic plastic, making them ceremony men, dispensers of idealism, deliverers and delivery boys employed to service religious need. One can begin to see why inside this crucible pastors, dislocated from the life of the church as fullness, begin to lose touch with themselves and creation reality. Leaders in our current church construct cannot win. Whichever way they move the platonic wall meets them. If they move outside of the ideal script they will not be listened to and if they keep on with the script, they initially might get more of a following, but over time will no longer be heard by a people addicted to the ideal and made immune to the real. Is it any wonder we are seeing so much dismay among the ranks of our leaders and so little real change in the heart of the people? They say that only one in twenty of pastors who commence the ministry will be there at retirement age. It's certainly not a job for the faint hearted! One wonders whether in its present form, it is meant to be a job at all.

The church culture in which all of this is happening increasingly lives for its own sake, and of late for its own survival. A friend summed up the place we have reach painfully well. Jesus, he said, wanted us to be in the world but not of it. The problem is that we have succeeded in neither. We are not in the world, but instead find ourselves in a church subculture removed from it. And inside that subculture we have become worldly. Every Sunday we demand infotainment and related activities to keep us coming and keep us happy. The platonic agenda has worked its way through the Western mind to ensure that the ideal image has become more apparently real than the real. It is this agenda that has triumphed over the Western and Christian mind and it has used the preaching event to assist that triumph. The immense gift of the Word has been taken and used to make the sons and daughters dependent on hearing, passive in doing and impotent in living as God intended they live.

The Word of God is losing its power in the very place where its power is meant to be greatest, in the lives of those it was given to empower and release into creation. It's no wonder that George Bana, a church commentator, says that the organised church in North America has only three to five years to reinvent itself or be consigned to cultural oblivion. That statement was made three years ago now. Inside this declining culture are a whole lot of people trying to live life and do the will of God. These are still very much the focus of the divine and eternal strategy. Let's look at how these sons and daughters are faring inside our increasingly dysfunctional ecclesiastic pods.

Chapter 9

The Heart Desires, Creatures and Creation

Idealism ensures that the truth preached from the pulpit remains, for the most part, too far above and away from where the saints really live. They cannot reach it and thus ultimately they cannot take it home. This arrangement generates a culture in which people work hard and long with passion and loyalty to build an organisation that cannot bring them into their inheritance in creation. The reason being that their inheritance is not in view in these churches; rather it is the inheritance of the church that is the focus. The effect of this hits home in the heart of every saint. The platonic ploy has worked hard to ensure that the heart desire of the sons and daughters does not come to the fore in the divine strategy. Satan knows the power of this heart and rightly fears what might happen if it were ever permitted to join with the created order. To create confusion by erecting generational strongholds between the saints, the Father and the creation is key to his agenda.

In the very beginning the serpent came to Eve with an offer that promised an ideal short cut to less than nowhere. You shall be like God, he said. Don't bother with all of this growth towards the fullness stuff, collecting little bits of wisdom along the way, working hard over so many years to subdue the creation. Just take the fruit. It looks great and tastes better. Satan pushed against Eve's capacity to doubt she had what it took to grow up in all things and thus fill up and out the image of God in which she had been made. Hence the offer of easy fruit, a single and definite bite that could take her direct to the divine was too hard to resist. The magnificence of the tree of the knowledge of good and evil must have made her wisdom feel so feeble by comparison. The certainty of the apparently knowledge-able serpent must have made her own vulnerability and innocence seem so childish and naive. So she took the offer and ate and then sold the ideal to her husband. Ever since that time ideal offers have been used to dislocate the image bearers from the creation mandate, stopping them from growing up in all things towards the fullness. It's time that we gave our answer to the serpent.

The heartbeat of the divine strategy is the individual heart desire of the saint. God placed within that heart – the thinking, feeling, deciding core of our being – the key to the creation purpose. Into the heart of every heart God breathed good desire, desire that he ever waits and wants to fulfil. In 2 Thessalonians 1:11–12 we read:

> To this end we also pray for you always that our God may count you worthy of your calling and fulfil every desire for goodness and the work of faith with power; in order that the name of our Lord Jesus may be glorified in you and you in him, according to the grace of our God and the Lord Jesus Christ.

I commented on these verses in *The Church Beyond the Congregation*:

> As we can see from these verses, the focus is definitely on the individual saints doing the works that make an impact. Looking into the hearts of these called-out people we find that there exists a powerful river called desire moving them to good

work. Specifically we find there a wellspring named 'desire for goodness'. This phrase about individual desire is placed right at the centre of a very impressive list of events and persons. In this passage the saints' 'calling' is in view. God intends that his purpose for our lives will move through our good desire to ultimately arrive in (and be expressed through) all of our 'works'. This work is characterised by a living and active 'faith' and is backed up by the Spirit's 'power'. It is these works, breathed into by a desire for goodness, which reveal the name and glory of Christ 'in you' and 'you in' Christ. This work, 'glorifying' the Son, in turn reveals the Father of heaven above. Such verses, and others like them, speak clearly of the powerful place the inner or personal desires and dreams of the saints have in the divine strategy. God intends that the good works of the saints come not so much from without; rather they are to be inspired and drawn from the deep of good desire. It is these heart desires for good that God intends to fuel and ignite all of the works of the saint. God did not come to empower his Word or his precious Spirit; they are already exalted, along with his name, above the heavens. Nor did he come to primarily validate the role of church leadership and the organisations they build. All these only serve their God-given purpose in equipping, releasing and empowering the life and work of the saints.

James Thwaites, *The Church Beyond the Congregation*, pp. 235f.

The cry of creation for liberation from its bondage to decay can only be heard in the human heart. The good desire God placed within that heart is the only created thing able to respond to and answer that cry. Within the heart's desire is the power of divine love. This gift and expression of God is given to enable us to embrace and join with every facet of our inheritance in creation. Our heart desire is called forth by the creation. It is focused by and arrives in every good work in creation. And it is fuelled and energised by the love of all created things. The deep and eternal sound of the

Father, spoken of in Romans 8:26, arrives in the good desire of the heart. Hence the work of the enemy down through history to dislocate and detach this heart from the divine heart beat of the eternal purpose. There are two things in particular that he has used to achieve this work. The first was idolatry and the second was idealism. These, as we shall see, are two peas from the same philosophical pod, close relatives that partner in the same satanic crime.

Instinctual life

Platonic idealism is essentially just a more sophisticated form of idolatry. To help unpack this statement we need to cover again some of the philosophical territory traversed in chapter 4. As mentioned there, Plato's ideal version of the transcendent realm does not exist. Hence, when one actually tries to describe it, one cannot. Actual transcendence is not expressible – it being outside of the immanence and thus beyond the reach of any finite contemplation. So, to convince us that his ideal/transcendent realm did exist, Plato had to make it look tangible. He had to give us the feeling that we could in fact identify with it; that it was almost, but not quite, within our reach. To achieve this counterfeit he used things in creation that could best approximate the ideal. These things had to be able to take on the appearance of being absolute, fixed, complete; in effect they had to look like they had arrived at perfection akin to the divine. To achieve this Plato made use of the conceptual and rational dimension of life.

After the Fall the serpent followed the same basic plan, but, rather than abstract reason, he used the creatures God had made to set up his ideal trap. The reasons for this were as follows. These creatures contained the attributes, nature and power of God in accordance with the level of glory in creation they occupied. Hence they expressed the divine person in certain ways. Also they expressed in certain ways the attributes, nature and power that were to be found in the image bearer. This enabled humankind to better identify with them, which was another plus for the enemy's agenda. The third and most strategic reason for their use by the serpent was the way in which they as creatures were substantially regulated in their behaviour by instinct.

The creatures were more fixed and predictable in their nature than humankind. Humanity does, of course, have an instinctual part to its nature, but we are more strongly characterised by our ability to choose and our ability to create. We are not made to live predominantly in and from the instinctual part of our nature. This is what makes us so strong at certain points and so weak in others. It creates the vulnerability that Adam and Eve no doubt felt when they looked over the Garden fence at the wild creation on the other side. We are not as majestic as the eagle in flight, as cunning as the tiger in the hunt, as free as the dolphin in the sea, as swift as the horse in movement. We can draw inspiration and wisdom from their attributes, but we are always both more than and less than them. We are not made to occupy a fixed place in creation. We are designed to keep moving and growing in, through and over all the things of creation. The calling on our lives is to gather wisdom from every attribute of every created thing and draw them up into our stewardship over the works of God's hands. Our arrival point is not in the instinctual or elemental things of earth. Rather our fullness is found in the heavens above the earth, our rule and our reach extending from earth right through to those heavens.

This was the creation purpose. Then came the choice and the dislocation. The easy offer of direct passage to arrival was a lie that, when accepted, came with dire consequence. The powerful attributes found in the creatures of instinct no longer inspired us to move out across the vast earth. Instead, the enemy used them to capture and contain our hearts. When you dislocate from God, you dislocate from the creation purpose. The upshot of this is that the very elements we were supposed to use as stepping stones to increasing levels of glory, now stand and step all over us. Why then did humanity so quickly come under the rule of elemental and instinctual things?

When humankind dislocated from God he found that what was once the freedom to choose now felt like rootlessness and a lack of certainty. What was once a freedom to mature and grow now felt like a lost cause and lack of identity. The things that were meant to be our greatest strength as the image bearer felt more like an acute weakness. So, humanity's response, as creatures of instinct, was to seek refuge in the strongest thing we could see; hence the move spoken of in Romans from the worship of the creator to that of the creature. The instinctual is strong; we are not. The creature has arrived; we have not. The creature knows the cycles of the seasons and matches them with ease; we are nomads often at the mercy of nature. The birds that feed and fly look so content; we are restless, yearning and wanting. The instinctual was fixed, complete, strong and absolute; people therefore forsook their own feeble heart and attached themselves to the apparent strength and certainty it offered.

Idol upgrade

The same addiction to the idol has continued down to this day. The serpent's action in the Garden was no different to what he did via Plato in the fifth century BC. The ideal other was simply upgraded to match the move in Israel (precipitated by the judgement of exile) away from idolatry to a more consistent monotheism; hence the statement: platonic idealism is just a more sophisticated form of idolatry. Plato simply moved our attachment to the instinctual away from the creature and to the conceptual. As such, idols were no longer feathered, furry or of wood and stone. Now they were made of pure, invisible thought. The idol as ideal was no longer earthy, tangible and present; it was now spiritual, abstract and future-oriented. It still, however, retained the quality so necessary to Satan, i.e. the fixed, arrived, absolute and complete feel. Adding strength to this new version of instinctual life was the (apparent) attachment of the ideal to the transcendent realm. We had upgraded from idols and animals to ideals and eternals, but essentially the old operating system had remained very much in place.

Down through history the best way to house, protect and express the idol or the ideal has been the authority construct. Priests aligned to rulers have generally always spoken for the dumb idol. In the Roman Empire these were joined as one in Caesar. Throughout subsequent history the emperor, king, state or institution has held, on behalf of the people, the right to own and thus speak for the idol or the ideal. The apparent reality that the idol or the ideal contains is used to justify the right of the authority construct to exist and exercise its power. Idealism is a catalyst for institutionalism and the institution is a catalyst for idealism. It has always been a very convenient marriage. One, as we shall see, that produces a powerful offspring named ideology.

We have come a long way from the days when pharaoh was declared divine and thus determined the life and fate of so many. Now the most powerful construct on the planet is the corporation and the most powerful form of idealism is consumerism. The church has kept well in step with the journey of the ideal – generally mimicking and, whenever possible, marrying the power brokers as they moved from empire, to state, to institution, to corporation. When future life idealism predominated the church was more necessary to the emperors and monarchs. However, from the post-war years to the 1960s, when present life idealism came into vogue, the church found itself without a societal date. To survive in the prior centuries it had formulated a strong Enlightenment approach to truth and hence had offered a somewhat Enlightenment version of God in and from its pulpits. Postmodernism and the loss of Enlightenment/Modern certainty about the existence of absolute and rational truth caught the church by surprise. It took a few decades for the new version to arrive. When it did it looked a lot like a corporate construct fitted for the consumer world. It was heavy with the vision thing, strong on leadership and had much product and many services on offer to help, heal and improve the lifestyle of those who joined.

Ever since the Garden the enemy has concentrated on dislocating the human heart from the divine purpose. He has ever sought to locate the focal point of life outside of the image bearer in some idol, construct, ideal, vision or leader – anywhere but in the individual heart. He has, for the greater part, always succeeded. Human desire cannot emerge in a culture or a construct that is fixed on the idol or the ideal. The reason being that in such settings human desire is made subservient to the agenda of the ideal or idol that defines and justifies the existence of the institution. The desire of the organisation ultimately eclipses the desire of the individual. To choose to forego individual desire to serve a larger corporate purpose may, to one degree or another, be appropriate in say a company selling product or an army at war. Indeed, this is why company and army motifs are so much in vogue in churches nowadays. However, it is another matter altogether when leaders take charge of a broader culture and commandeer the works, and thus desires, of people within it. The record of history clearly shows that whenever leaders and their social/political visions are installed at the centre of a culture with a view to managing the people towards the realisation of that vision, then much dysfunction and great damage ensues. Such, I believe, is the case with our current way of being church.

The church as construct, as much as good people do good things within it, has been predominately formed and fashioned by platonic idealism. To attract and hold its following it has become central to the kingdom process, fixed as a construct on the landscape and attached to an idealised version of reality removed from life. Its leaders, if they are to succeed, increasingly have to act and perform like idealised creatures of instinct – dynamic, fixed, visionary and arrived. If the local church and its leader are not all of this, or do not at least appear to approximate them, then the frail, wandering, disorganised, incomplete people will find themselves at sea. If kept there too long they will begin to paddle hard to the next ecclesiastic pontoon offering them security and shelter from the storms of life. We have become so accustomed to the strong, fixed and ideal-housing centre named the local church, that we do not question its existence. It is time we acknowledged how much of our current way of being church derives from platonic idealism.

Heaven's frail focus

The focus of heaven is not the Word, it is not the Spirit, it is not the preacher or the local church on the corner – the focus of heaven is the frail heart of saints presently beating far below the surface of so much that has layered over and laid them low. To submerge the heart and make it the servant of something other is to effectively immobilise the power of human desire and greatly diminish the life that comes from its love. When this happens we no longer look into our heart for the way ahead, rather we are glued to the ideal, pre-occupied with the next adjustment we need to make us appear to be like it. The person we are becomes fixed on becoming the person we are not. We are made dependent on a thing that is not and thus held back from fulfilling the divine purpose. Our love for others comes from our heart. This love is carried by good desire and expressed in the good works (deeds) we give to others. If our heart desire goes off-line then our work cannot convey our love to others. The effects of this are serious and many; not the least of which is the way that it impacts on our relationship with God. As John said: 'No one has beheld God at any time; if we love one another, God abides in us, and his love is perfected in us. God is love, and the one who abides in love abides in God, and God abides in him' (1 Jn. 4:12, 16). If the enemy can suppress love by taking it off-line then he has won a great victory over the image bearer.

I am aware of course that most leaders do not head out to create constructs that get in the way of the kingdom process, but it appears that there is something in the system that seems to take this route apart from such a desire. I spoke with a fellow recently, a church leader of a newly formed fellowship. The people, he said, had come from various settings – around 40 per cent new Christians, 40 per cent coming directly (or more recently) from other fellowships and 20 per cent who had at one time in the past been in Christian fellowship. As a leader he knew the need for gathering and community and was encouraging and facilitating the same. This process had been going on now for around eighteen months and already the dynamic was changing. In particular the 40 per cent coming more directly from other fellowships were calling for more input into their lives from the leadership. They wanted the leaders to supply ministries, activities and resource to meet their spiritual needs. In particular many had begun to ask about the vision of the church – speaking more and more about the need to decide on one, to write it down and clearly communicate it to those on the inside and those thinking about coming in.

The fellow said that the new Christians didn't want any of this; they were just enjoying the community. It was those whose expectations had already been set in place by other fellowships who were pushing the process towards a centrist way of church. Already this leader was seeing a community of individuals in relationship move to define a centre and a vision that worked to produce things to serve the religious and social needs of the people. He was looking at a movement from community to institution happening right before his eyes. And, as much as he was trying to resist that tendency, he felt he was being drawn, sometimes overtly and sometimes by stealth, towards taking charge of yet another church as construct.

We believe as church leaders that our institution is serving the needs of the people and thus enabling them to do the will of God and live for him. However, the record of minimal impact and the extent of dysfunction in most local churches seem to suggest that our best-laid plans are not hitting the intended mark. The church as institution attracts the following it does firstly because there are not many other options currently presenting themselves. Also, and more critical to our present discussion, it attracts people because of the way in which it aligns with the platonic approach to reality. People demand a strong and fixed centre, because Plato has created a propensity in human nature towards such fixed ideal focal points. This is why the move towards the church as construct, as much as one might try and resist it – via say cells, variations in meeting times and places or controlled releases into market-place ministries

– settles in like inclement weather every time. Even these very moves to resist certification are still engineered from a centre, causing even new and novel things to ultimately still refer back to it. As the saying goes, all roads lead to Rome – the reason being because they were built by Rome for that very purpose.

Well-tensioned and non-ideal life

We are made for creation and should not be attached to fixed centres that house the ideal. The fullness waiting in creation can only be reached by going into the relational and good working our way through the thorns. Such a journey means a life of tension, unresolved tension that keeps us ever reaching out for more in life and more in God. It carries us into times of pain and yearning, times of hope unmet and despair deep-felt, times of joy and sadness. Paul speaks of this way of life. He tells us that there will be times when we will be popular and times when we are nobody, there will be times when people are saying bad things about us and times when good reports are circulating about us, seasons of glory and those of dishonour, days when we feel we have nothing and days when we feel that our heart can embrace all things. It is the lack we feel, the vulnerability of our heart that gives us ability to keep growing, feeling, relating and reaching for the high call in life.

We cannot love an ideal; neither can an ideal love us. Love is a creation exchange between those things that are real and living. One might think that one is loving an ideal vision, construct or leader, but such a feeling, for the most part, is only an experience of pining in relation to the gulf between where you are and where you are told you should be. Idealism is the counterfeit of intimacy. It makes us paupers, daily begging for bread that falls stale from the table of the ideologues. The outcome of the platonic ploy is that we, as saints, do not follow the course of our heart desire into creation. The reasons being that we are not looking in the direction of creation for our inheritance to come and we do not think that our heart desires really matter. Such leaves us dependent on the construct, ever waiting for the ideal it promises to arrive. It leaves our heart desires confused, dammed up rather than river running to the land we were made to dwell upon. The land is dry, we are suppressed and kept inside and there is little light and life to those in darkness and death.

If the heart desire of the sons and daughters does not connect with creation's cry then we have a no show in regard to the eternal purpose. Paul, by the Spirit, said that we are heirs of the Father and joint heirs with the Son. He then added that such would only happen if we suffered with the Son. This suffering is the feeling of heart's desire for inheritance touching creation's yearning for fullness. The heart pain we must feel is the pain of travail. From the heart comes desire, from desire comes love, from love comes pain – pain that is travail, travail that heads into birth. The salt, light and love that must emerge from the sons and daughters to touch this world can only come via the way of suffering. As in the beginning, anything, anyone, any serpent that keeps us from that needs to be taken out of the way.

Peter the apostle said of those who live like creatures of instinct that such made them ripe to 'be captured and killed' (2 Pet. 2:12). The human heart, identified with the organ first formed in the child of the womb, the organ that joins breath to blood to give life to the body, has been imprisoned by platonic idealism and is being killed. If we are ever to answer the cry of a waiting creation we must cast out the leaven of Plato and allow God to bring us through to life and work under a Hebrew sky. It's time that the rule and reign of platonic dualism in the Christian Church came to an end. To break from its bars of steel will take more than sermons and alternative service formats; it will take death. Not just any death. It will take the divine dying that Jesus the Christ gave us as a gift through his incarnation, death and resurrection.

The human heart can achieve what the church, as construct, cannot. The reason it can is closely related to the reason why the construct cannot, that being, the heart lives and the construct does not. This heart is frail and breathing, the construct is fixed and impervious. This heart is designed to move with the finite good towards the fullness. The construct is designed to move away from the good towards the ideal. The only creation reality that exists in a construct is the reality of the life of people it holds. Let's make a way for this heart by taking away the construct that presently keeps it inside. We are born to rise through the elemental and instinctual things to the fullness – there to steward the creation under wings of wisdom grown through choice, desire and travail. To accomplish this we must strip back the nice, proper and civil layers that have encased the platonic stronghold in religion. We must go to the heart of the platonic agenda and decode the DNA the serpent has so effectively used to infect the body of humanity. To do this we need to look directly into the ultimate plan that Plato had when he set up his philosophy. We need to look at Plato's agenda to set up the rule of ideology over the human person and the human process.

We have a choice before us. It's basically the same choice we have had before us in the Garden. Will we go the way of creation or the way of the idol? Will we rule and steward the all things of creation or will we stay under the rule of elemental things? The choice to go the way of creation rather than the way of the corporation will not be easily taken. There is only one road on offer to get there. If we are to arrive in the new landscape and give our answer to the serpent we must take the way of divine death. To know the direction that death takes, we need to know just what it is we need to die to. To my mind just what this is is more clearly in view now than it has been for many centuries.

Chapter 10

The DNA Down at the Church Centre

We need to consider the historical contexts in which Plato's philosophy emerged if we are to understand his agenda. I noted in *The Church Beyond the Congregation* how the move away from present-world idolatry towards other-realm idealism happened during the same period that Israel was purged of idolatry via the judgement of exile. Plato in the West and Buddha in the East both broke away from the idol and posited an ideal realm only accessible via pure thought and contemplation. I believe that this move away from idolatry towards idealism could have been Satan's response to the events that were happening in Israel.

Going further now into the more immediate context in which Plato lived and developed his philosophy, we arrive in Athens, Greece during the period 427–347 BC. During his life Plato experienced political turmoil and wars. In his early years Athens was ruled by a tribal aristocracy, of which Plato's family was a part. This rule by aristocrats broke down and was replaced by the rule of democracy – a system strongly opposed to the rule of royals or demagogues. Democratic Athens fought a long and terrible war against Sparta during the time of Plato's youth. At that time a tribal aristocracy ruled Sparta. This war lasted for twenty-eight years and brought with it famines, plagues, the fall of Athens, civil war and a rule of terror, which was called rule of the Thirty Tyrants – two of the leaders of which were Plato's uncles (of aristocratic lineage). The tyrants were finally overthrown and democracy re-established. This democratic rule did not, how-ever, mean a return to stability or safety for Athens or Plato. It was during this rule that Socrates was sentenced to death. Plato's life was also in danger at this time; he left Athens as a consequence and, among other destinations, sojourned at Sicily, where it appears he was involved in some degree of political intrigue. He finally returned to Athens, set up the school and penned the works for which he is famous.

It is important to understand that the philosophy of idealism did not develop in a political or social vacuum. The worldview that has been the single most powerful influence on the Western and Christian mind came from a critical time in the history of the divine plan. It also emerged from a young aristocrat whose life had been strongly traumatised by the destruction of a system in which his family had held a privileged position. As the name of the work that Plato is famous for suggests – *The Republic* – Plato's agenda in putting forth his philosophy of idealism and dualism was social and political. He was not a free-thinking, otherworldly sage living humbly in a monastery. He was a man of privilege and ambition, living in a city that has powerfully influenced the course of human development. It could be said that what Jerusalem is for religion, Athens is for humanism. In this light, let's look again at the platonic philosophy. From there we will un-cover the serpent's agenda enacted in and through its divided worldview.

By way of summary of Plato's theory of forms and ideals, I include here a quote from Karl Popper:

The things in flux, the degenerate and decaying things, are (like the state) the offspring, the children, as it were, of perfect things. And like children, they are copies of their original primogenitors. The father or original of a thing in flux is what Plato calls its 'Form' or its 'Pattern' or its 'Idea'. As before, we must insist that the Form or Idea, in spite of its name, is no 'idea in our mind'; it is not a phantasm, nor a dream, but a real thing. It is, indeed more real than all the ordinary things which are in flux, and which, in spite of their apparent solidity, are doomed to decay; for the Form or Idea is a thing that is perfect, and does not perish. The Forms or Ideas must not be thought to dwell, like perishable things, in space and time. They are outside space and also outside time (because they are eternal). But they are in contact with space and time; for since they are the primogenitors or models of the things which are generated, and which develop and decay in space and time, they must have been in contact with space at the beginning of time.

Karl Popper, *The Open Society and its Enemies. Volume 1. Plato*, p. 25

In chapter five we looked at the platonic move from idea to ideal. Let's now take a look at how the platonic agenda makes the move from ideal to ideology. Plato set up a situation that would necessitate a particular response. He created a problem that would call forth a solution designed by him. It's a well-known political ploy; create a predicament and then offer a tailor-made solution to it – a solution that just happens to require your services. Plato established a world in which there existed a removed, fixed and eternal status quo, one that no finite being could directly access or change. It logically followed on from this that because that ideal realm was real and this present world was not, then people would need to have someone or something in place that could access the ideal on their behalf.

The vehicle that Plato had in mind for this job was the 'State' and the ruler he had in mind to take charge of that state was 'the philosopher king'. In fact the whole of the Republic can be seen as Plato's less than subtle attempt to put himself forward to Athens as a wise and noble (one might even say ideal) aristocrat, ready, if invited, to take the reigns of power and rule the people. The State, ruled by the likes of Plato, would be the most suitable vehicle for the job because it was best able to approximate the ideal realm and transmit its reality to the people of that State. It could be established 'thought', fixed by law and be trusted, unlike the people, to remain true to the ideal from whence it came because it was not human and changeable. For Plato, the State, even though it was of this present realm and thus not perfect, was the highest and best expression of good that finite and corrupted individuals could experience. As such, it was the finest suitor to occupy the centre and, with some help from the best available philosopher king at the time, rule the people.

Once the State was in place a status quo would be established that would be extremely hard for anyone to budge. Plato's philosophical justification for the rigid fixedness of his State system derives from his definition of 'good'. In the Republic 'good' is explained as everything that preserves and 'evil' as everything that destroys or corrupts.

> This view is used for evaluating the general trend and main directions of all changes in the world of sensible things. For if the starting point of all change is perfect and good (already arrived), then change can only be a movement that leads away from the perfect and good; it must be directed towards the imperfect and the evil, towards corruption.
>
> Karl Popper, *The Open Society and its Enemies. Volume 1. Plato*, p. 36

This meant that any variation or move away from the absolute, an absolute that just happened to be defined by the State, was a corruption. Thus, once in place, the ruling institution could argue, on the basis of its version of the way things are, that anyone suggesting change or agitating for the new was an evil person. And they, being evil, could not (by platonic definition) be representing something good. Once you set up rules that suit your own agenda, and convince people that they are divine rules, then it is very hard for the people to manoeuvre – unless of course they do so in line with the maze you have set up for them.

The idea that came to rule

Platonic philosophy creates an immense need that can only be filled by its own agenda. It convinces us that reality is something removed from our life in creation. It takes a hold of shared ideas and human desires and attaches their arrival or fulfilment to its own version of the eternal realm. To help feeble humans access this fabricated realm it sets up an authority construct and places it at the centre of their community. Over this institution it then places leaders who possess, by birth or by calling, the divine 'right to rule' the people from that centre. Once the authority construct is in place it is deemed, by virtue of its position, to be the good and any variation to it is defined as aberrant and thus evil. It is able to live fat, ever increasing its authority by feeding itself on the hunger, fear and addiction it has induced in people's lives because it appears to supply their need for meaning, security and significance. In this way Plato set up a version of reality that enabled the elite few to take hold of a creation idea, attach it to the ideal realm and use its now twisted power to take charge of the masses. From idea, to ideal to ideology the platonic agenda works to ensure that the elite at the centre, the possessors of the ideal, will take and hold power over people. This is its DNA, this is its plan, this is the reason why the platonic worldview came into being and has been so powerfully used down through history to serve the enemy's purpose.

This agenda is clearly set out in *The Republic* and is best expressed most starkly in the following quote from Plato's pen:

> The greatest principle of all is that nobody, whether male or female, should ever be without a leader. Nor should the mind of anybody be habituated to letting him do anything at all on his own initiative, neither out of zeal, or even playfully. But in war and in the midst of peace to his leader he shall direct his eye, and follow him faithfully. And even in the smallest matters he should stand under leadership. For example, he should get up, or move, or wash, or take his meals . . . only if he has been told to do so . . . In a word, he should teach his soul, by long habit, never to dream of acting independently, and to become utterly incapable of it. In this way the life of all will be spent in total community. There is no law, nor will there ever be one, which is superior to this, or better and more effective in ensuring salvation and victory in war. And in times of peace, and from the earliest childhood on should it be fostered, this habit of ruling others, and of being ruled by others. And every trace of anarchy should be utterly eradicated for all the life of all the men, and even of the wild beasts which are subject to men.

Karl Popper, *The Open Society and its Enemies. Volume 1. Plato*, p. 103.

Popper's comments on these startling words are perhaps the best initial comment that can be made:

> Never was a man more in earnest in his hostility towards the individual. And this hatred is deeply rooted in the fundamental dualism of Plato's philosophy; he hated the individual and his freedom just as he hated the varying particular experiences,

the variety of the changing world of sensible things. In the field of politics, the individual is to Plato the Evil One himself.

Karl Popper, *The Open Society and its Enemies. Volume 1. Plato*, pp. 103f.

Speaking of future interpretations of Plato's intensions in the Republic by religious and humanist alike, Popper says that 'this attitude, as anti-humanitarian and anti-Christian as it is, has been consistently idealised'. Considering Plato's intent, is it any wonder that so many have tended toward such idealism?

Plato plainly states the objective he set out to achieve when he introduced his philosophy to humanity. This is the mindset that has most powerfully influenced the course of Western and Christian history. In Plato's plan the image bearers are not free to grow up in all things. They are not served by truth and by leaders so that they can realise the good desire of their heart in and through their good work in creation. Rather they are fixed to the ideal, kept under control and rendered unable to move this way or that unless it suits their leader. It sounds a lot like the devil we know, does it not? When contrasted with the creation mandate that calls us to grow, create and discover our way in, through and over all things, this fixed state of attachment to the ideal and the authority construct that houses it is seen for what it is – a worldview and social agenda diametrically opposed to what God had in heart and mind when he made the image bearers.

'But surely truth is fixed and not subject to change and also it is one with the eternal and transcendent God?' In response to such a query I note again the way in which Plato mimicked the creation reality to gain fuel for his philosophy. Further to this, revisiting some of the ground covered in chapter four, I include here another note regarding the transcendence and immanence issue. Yes, transcendent reality in God is fixed and eternal. However we do not live in relation to that transcendence. We live in relation to the immanence of God in creation. Within the created order God gave us moral law and other truths that cannot change. He has also done many things, the incarnation, the atonement and the like that establish realities that cannot be altered. These givens, however, were never meant to fix in place a status quo that ruled our lives and gave us no room to move unless we did so in obedience or direct response to them.

The truths of God are not ultimately known by fixed rational thought, they are known in relationship with God and creation. Reason is a part of that knowing, but it does not occupy, as the Enlightenment mind claimed, the fixed and ideal centre of truth. Truth has no one fixed centre. Truth is God in the immanence in relationship with our lives. As such truth breathes, moves, converses and unfolds its layers and levels of glory as we journey with it to the fullness. The relational expression and experience of truth is alone able to contain reason, morality, goodness, tension, knowing and more. It is both strong and vulnerable, powerful and weak, perfect but open to our entering in and through it. This living truth can travel into wisdom, igniting the good desire of heart, moving us to good work and traverse the vast spaces of life waiting to be filled. Truth is designed and gifted by God to ensure we have maximum ability and full finite freedom to gather our inheritance in, through and over all things.

Plato has counterfeited truth and used that counterfeit to keep the image bearer fixed, immobilised and unable to answer the cry of creation. This ensures that any institution built according to platonic specifications cannot ultimately equip people to engage creation and gain their inheritance. The reason being that everything encoded in the platonic and satanic DNA that infects these institutions works to ensure the opposite. The first centre in history was the Tower of Babel. It was a well-organised apparent short cut to the heavens that kept everybody busy and stopped them from spreading out across the earth in fulfilment of the creation mandate. From that day to this, humankind has looked to someone or something to take up residence in the centre on their behalf. Only with such a centre in place could people feel strong, secure, organised and aligned to the ideal ever dangled before them by those in power.

Israel was not created with a political centre; it was made of families and clans who worked the land. God gave prophets, judges and his very own rule to help serve this society. It was not, however, enough; the Israelites wanted a centre just like the nations around them. So they started a lobby group and finally got their man, who was called king. In this rush to the centre, they did not reject the prophet or the judge; rather, as God said to Samuel, they rejected the rule of God himself. Some good, of course, did come with the monarchy. However, it ultimately caused Israel to fail in the divine purpose. The monarchy led the people into endemic idolatry and ultimately into the judgement of exile from the land.

The first of the platonic leavened constructs in the Christian era was the Roman Catholic Church. This came into being on the back of the early church's vigorous use of Plato to validate its truth claims against the attacks on Christianity by Greek philosophers. Once the virus was in the system it fixed itself to the dogma, the structure and the culture of the church. From there it spread to the Holy Roman Empire and, via the Renaissance and Reformation, to one degree or another, to every Western religious and humanist institution or movement that followed.

Thank God I am not like other ideologues

When we hear the word ideology perhaps Communism and Fascism come immediately to mind. However, we do need to be careful; we should not stop and say, like the Pharisee of old, thank God I am not like other men. The history of the church demonstrates that it has little or no immunity to this platonic virus. It is in fact more highly infected than other institutions because it owes its existence to the special relationship it has with transcendent and divine reality and was the major carrier of the platonic virus into the West. We have looked at many of the elements that make for the local church construct – its orientation away from creation towards the eternal and transcendent; its existence as something separate to that of individual saints; its occupation of the centre of (and thus the rule over) the kingdom people and process; its use of vision and idealism to attract and keep a following. For anyone to say that Plato has not influenced the way this institution is structured is to stretch credulity a long way. If we, as the church, think that we are immune to the platonic virus, that we are free from its influence, then we are being foolish in the extreme. No one is immune to it, least of all those who consider themselves, by virtue of their spiritual standing and learning, untainted and untouched. It is only by acknowledging the presence of platonic leaven in our culture, and thus in the institutions that express that culture, that we can begin to counter its influence. If we deny its influence then we are many times more prone to be ruled by it.

There is definitely something strong and fixed, sitting at the very heart of the institution of church – something we need to overcome if ever the church is to emerge and engage the creation as God intended. At the heart of the rule of ideology we do not find truth, rather, we find a stronghold, a way of thinking that came from the enemy of our souls. We need to face up to the fact that inside our local church constructs there exists a virus injected by the enemy. The disease and dysfunction this virus brings to the body of Christ has a long and tragic case history.

There is, however, an opportunity before us at this time, an invitation to face the generational strongholds that have held us bound to our church centres and kept from the creation inheritance.

Scripture speaks in Revelation of the deeds of the Nicolaitans (2:6, 15). The word is telling, in that the two words that make the composite are translated 'to conquer or rule the people'. This age old tendency for an elite with knowledge and power to take control over the group no doubt found expression in the early church. John (the writer of the Revelation) speaks of a Diotrephes, 'who loves to be first among' the people of God. His actions, described in 3 John 9, 10 indicate that he was well and truly a fellow who loved and lived to occupy the centre. To my mind the term Nicolaitans is a useful word to describe the stronghold that the evil one uses to bring disease and dysfunction to the body of humanity and, more specifically, to the body of Christ.

Unless we deal with the platonic virus infecting our system, any surface changes will continue to have little, if any effect. We can keep moving our chairs and our choirs, be extreme and radical in worship, meet in smaller rooms or only once a month, get an amazing band or an incredible preacher, but the cry in the spheres of creation engaged by work will remain unanswered. People living and working in health, education, business, government, recreation, in the spheres of marriage and family, will remain unmoved by whatever intense activity we put on inside our ideal construct. Our society, captured as it is by idealism and ideology, will remain ever immune to our own lesser version of the same. If the body of Christ has anything to offer a world held under by the rule of idealism, it will have to break through the platonic stronghold itself. If it does not then it will have nothing real to offer, it will have no light to attract those trapped under the rule of elemental things.

Hence the choice before us at this time; the choice between the corporation or the creation, between the uniformity of one man's vision or the diversity of every person's heart desire, between the rule of the leader and the life of the individual.

Don't burn the building

In *The Church Beyond the Congregation* I spoke about the strategic judgements that God put in place after the fall – the reality sign of thorns, sweat, futility and death that spoke to humanity of the true state of things in the heart. These thorns are not our enemy, they are our ally. Over the many years of human history we find that generational stronghold come into being in the very place that these thorns exist. In the place of our fear, our anger, our need for security and our selfishness strongholds in our mind form authority structures that either control or sanction (depending on who is trying to rule whom) these propensities. Among other things this means that institutions, be they local church or corporation, are not something entirely separate to us. Rather, they are a tangible expression of the way that we think. What the institution of church presently is constitutes the best indication and expression of who we as saints born in the West really are.

Any divine change in the nature of things, any judgement to set things right begins at the house of God. The institution does not define this house, it is known in heaven to be the people of God. Presently, however, these people are for the most part identified with the church as construct. As such, this expression contains and holds within itself many good people and good things. These, of course, we must not lose in our journey into the new landscape; hence the need to understand that the church as institution is not ultimately something other, but is rather a physical expression of generational strongholds that exist in our heart and mind. We can react and burn the building, however, as is the case in history, the revolutionary will soon become the new dictator. It is of no use to destroy an institution – it only creates rubble. We must, instead, destroy the generational strongholds that have taken up residence in our hearts. Only then will we be able to build again in the new landscape.

So, it is not a matter of walking away from the construct, or destroying it, or hating the leader of it. There may be a time to walk, but it should not be the first and easy option we take. If we react we will only carry the same old strongholds with us through the rest of our life. The church as construct carries within it divine authority, as did the empire ruled by Nero. If we react and run or turn and burn the construct, then we will be in effect turning against the attributes, nature and power of God presently held within it. It is for this reason we need to work decidedly to transition the church as institution. We need to see the DNA sitting at its centre carried into death. This is the best and only hope we have of change as individual saints and hence of change as his body, the church.

In the new landscape there will of course be leaders, elders, ministry gifts and places, large and small, in which we can gather. Again, these things have never, of themselves, been our problem. The challenge before us is to release these elements and gifts from the ideological centre and see them woven into the fabric of every sphere of creation. I hasten to add here that none of this will occur ideally. Thank God for that! Again, if transition is to happen, then the platonic virus presently sitting strong and stubborn at the centre of the church as construct has to die. The church as construct is a host for the platonic virus, one that must be dispersed if we are ever to break free of infection. Only through the death of this DNA will we see the coalesced authority and resources inside our collapsing houses redeployed to serve the church as fullness.

After a chapter submerged in platonic syrup it is good to come up for some air! It is important to declare, with thanks, that our creator God is in, through and over all things and is well able to bring life and reality into whatever mind we are thinking with. Human desire and everyday life also keep on pushing their way to the surface of reality to command our attention, causing us to touch and encounter that which God has for us. We are not all totally lost in a platonic illusion with no sight, smell and sound of life. Imagine, however, if we came to a place where we could no longer be ruled by an ideal, a product, a man, a movement, a false future, a teaching – to a place where these elemental things no longer reigned, but rather served, as God intended them to serve, the image bearer? The power in these God-given things to fuel our journey into all that he has in and for us in creation is immense. We need them under our feet. We can no longer afford to have them over our head.

Many saints are sensing the judgement of God working its way through the body of Christ at this time. Certain ways of thinking and being church are coming to a close to make way for something new to emerge. A divine journey into death, via the judgement now coming on the house, is before us. This transition between the old and the new must be taken. It needs to be done with an eye on the thorns and the strongholds that amass around them and with an eye on the ability idealism has to take on any new form – Hebrew, Greek or Californian – to live to rule another day. We need ears to keep hearing what the Spirit is saying concerning the new creation church, a body of people God created, redeemed and determined would have no king, no centre, no master, except Jesus. Let's track this journey of judgement, of death and of change; knowing that the resurrection life in, through and over all things is only given to those who suffer and die with him.

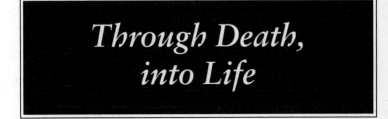

Through Death, into Life

Chapter 11

The Church – From Death to Life

'I gave you a king in my anger, and took him away in my wrath' (Hos. 13:11). This verse from Hosea is telling indeed, particularly in the light of what we have seen of the platonic agenda and its influence on our present way of being church. There came a time in Israel when God could no longer abide what had become of Israel under the rule of kings. There had been good rulers like David and Josiah, but ultimately the move towards a fixation of power at the centre and a containment of the divine purpose therein was inevitable. There comes that time when God decrees a change and moves to restore in line with his eternal purpose. He moves in judgement against the generational strong-holds that have become entrenched in the power structures over people's lives. I believe that we are in such a time of judgement and transformation.

We may look at our own church construct and believe, in comparison to certain others, that we are permitting sufficient freedom and release to happen. As such, we may think that this judgement will bypass our particular con-struct and deal only with 'the guilty ones'. However, the record of Scripture shows that when God moves he does so in relation to the entire body of Christ. He speaks and judges, as is evident in Revelation, to counsels that have set up residence in the entire body of a city or region. I don't believe any person can say they are free of platonic leaven and the control scenarios it brings with it. It will ultimately be in and through the time of judgement that we will be able to give an answer in relation to our own case. As the new emerges in the lives of those we lead and serve, we will be able to tell whether we value their freedom more than we do our leadership.

It was the Nicolaitan stronghold and the way of life it produced that God hated and moved to purge. He loved the people involved in that error, but as the great physician he will often heal by first wounding, cutting through to the cancer that has grown within. The platonic leaven presently sitting at the centre of the church as construct is now coming up for treatment. As such those aligned to it, in whatever degree, will feel the pain and experience the dying that comes with its judgement. Our thinking and our structures are infected. The divine temperature is on the way up. We must all feel the heat before this fever breaks and the body is free. It is God's love for us that moves him to prise us loose from the harmful things we attach ourselves to.

In certain sections of the Western church we are now seeing the strongest move towards the rule of leaders over people and process in centuries. Books on leadership and the power of their visions are best sellers. Conferences on apostles leading us into victory and new ways to socially engineer the saints into meeting after ministry after meeting increasingly dot the church landscape. One recent prayer letter from a prominent ministry spoke of thousands of saints lined up on the plain ready to do battle. Each one of the thronged masses, the blurb said, was able to recognise and respond to the voice of their own leader standing on the stage before them. Again, these communications come from the cutting edge and thus are more extreme examples.

They are, however, as mentioned, an indication of what we have in lesser form in every church stream and a signal of where things are heading.

When God moves to judge there is death and life in the process. A demolition and a building take place. The seed of the new season germinates in the earth under the old construct and begins to push its way to the surface. As it does, it signals the emergence of the new, which is used to accelerate the death of the old. This two-track or two-part process in the divine judgement is important to grasp if we are to better understand the season before us. The new seed rising up in the landscape is evidenced by increasing numbers of saints seeking to be the church in the sphere of creation they engage through work. These saints, moved by desire of heart, are joining with others to be and build the body of Christ in all of life. The character of this movement is still ambiguous, its strength is frail but promising, its motives are mixed and very human. Although aspects of this move are assisted and encouraged by church leaders, a good deal of it is happening without reference to the ecclesiastic construct.

In many ways the lack of congregation-based church leadership in the new move is, for the present, a good thing. It enables the saints emerging in this way to do so without over much intervention by the church as construct. It is often the case that when pastors discover marketplace ministries, they tend to implement programmes for business people that look a lot like their own church programme. They put on meetings, give teaching on leadership (often heavily laden with late 1980s corporate management principles) and spice the mix with encouragements to give to the ministry of the church. Whilst leaders are encouraging the saints to minister out there, they can be found leavening (sometimes in none to subtle ways) the new lump with old DNA.

This is the danger of the present. Many pastors, looking around for the next move, are heading out to extend the jurisdiction of their local church over the market place. The church as construct might think that it can simply enter into the new landscape, but it cannot. Ultimately it is culturally unable to penetrate the world of work in its present form. Even though it is trying, thankfully, it cannot move far enough from its ideal isolation in constant rounds of teaching and meeting before it is pulled back into ecclesiastic line. The elephant, as much as it might make a splash on impact, cannot swim with the ocean-going fish. God's ultimate intent is, of course, to create a seamless church, one body standing throughout creation. Hence the need to keep the church as construct somewhat at bay for a season – a season in which it can go through the divine dying necessary to make it a blessing to the church as fullness. There is no use bringing thinking and strategy that has not worked inside the church as construct into the new landscape. When the ministry gifts, which are presently tied into and identified with the church as construct, are ready for release into the new creation church, they will come as servants not masters. Until then they need to attend to the more pressing business at hand (i.e. divine dying and the dissolution of the centre that plays host to the platonic DNA). Thus, the new has to keep emerging and the old has to embrace death. These will join in God's good time.

One body, going through

I would not want to give the impression that these two facets of the church are categorically distinct and subject to different treatment. Rather they sit on either side of an equal sign in an equation that God is now resolving into one. It is helpful to look at the two facets so as to better understand them, but these, again, are one body under one eternal purpose. In reality most of those being stirred by the new are still identified in some way with a local or cell expression of church. Also, those who have made the move and no longer choose, for whatever reason, to identify with a local or cell expression of church, have done much business with the church as construct in the past. Hence, it is still a strong part of their thinking and often relational network; as such, it still determines many of their responses and/or reactions in regard to their Christian life. Even if we stand outside of the church as construct, we are still defining ourselves (albeit negatively) in relation to the construct we have left, i.e. it still has an influence over our identity and actions.

Many of the strongholds that caused the church as construct to rise on the plain in the first place still reside in the thinking, even of those who no longer identify with it. If these strongholds are not carried into death, individually and corporately, then they will in time begin to reappear, expressing themselves in new ways in the individual's work and relationships. If those with a heart for the new react, they may find initial freedom, but their resources will soon be depleted and their struggle against the powers in the spheres of creation will falter. We are one body and we must go through as one body. This is not a call to bland uniformity under one agenda; rather, it is a reminder of creation and divine reality. I am not prescribing what any individual should or should not do in regard to their relationship with the church as construct. Life is too complex to offer a solution in a sentence. However, we all must join in the same travail for the new.

The strongholds that exist in our minds find their most tangible expression and form in the constructs we build and identify with. As such, it is in the place of the church as construct that the most dramatic change will and must come for all of the body of Christ; both for those who presently identify with it and for those who don't. For this reason we need to track the journey of transition by the church as construct. There is much that can be said of the new landscape church now emerging, but that will not be the primary concern of the remainder of the book. In regards to the ground we have covered thus far pertaining to the platonic agenda, it is more important that we understand and embrace the way of judgement now coming on the church as construct. We will do this firstly in relation to the power structure that holds centre place in that construct. Then, in the following chapter, we will track the journey of the individual in transition. From there we will look at issues relating to the role of the church leader in transition and some perspectives in regard to their relationship to the church now emerging in the new landscape.

When you get there you'll know

What happens when one time gives way to the next; when one way of church enters into death and another emerges into life? What is the relationship between the old and the new during such a time of transition? What is the relationship between the individual's life and that of the corporate body in such times? These kinds of questions could go on and on; the answers to these and others like them are far from simple. I would not want to give the impression that what is to follow is the full or final word on the matter. One of the main reasons why easy answers cannot be given is because many of the questions concerning the new can only be fully answered by one's own heart. Answers will come as we reach the place where they can be drawn out from our engagement of life itself. Idealism drives us to imagine some arrival point before we commence the journey. It is our good desire that will bring into our lives the good that will then light up the steps ahead and so on from there. The answers we need along the way are waiting for us in the creation, in our inheritance, in the fullness. They are waiting for us to come and discover them as providence and choice permit.

We have been too programmed as saints to follow ten-point plans before we have had opportunity to locate our desire in regard to even the first step. We are too often given easy and neat closure at the end of sermons, made to feel the issue is wrapped up before we have even driven out of the church car park. For this season of change we need to take courage, embracing much more unresolved space and tension than perhaps we have been accustomed to. We are not simply changing the church programme. We are not just implementing the latest plan for success or crowd control. We are looking to tear down centuries-old strongholds that sit both in the citadel of our church and at the apex of our mind. We need to wean ourselves from the need to resolve and package truth so as to arrive in our heads a long time before our life has really changed. To see us through this time we need to decide to fellowship with Jesus as he journeys us through the necessary suffering into his divine death. Only in and through that journey will the life and wisdom we need for this time arise.

Trail-blazing Messiah

To enable us to take such a journey, it is essential that we look again at the trail blazed by the Son of God made man. Jesus Christ is our forerunner in all things. He came to open up a creation whose fullness had been enclosed in the judgement of thorns, sweat, futility and death. To do this he suffered his way through every one of these judgements and made a way through once again to our eternal inheritance in creation. This essential facet of the work of God in the incarnation was covered in some detail in *The Church Beyond the Congregation*. We can build on that understanding by considering Jesus' strategy in relation to the power structures that ruled over the people. When we seek to engage the creation to draw its fullness into our life and inheritance we must follow the same path that Jesus took.

Jesus faced, like any other person, the thorns God himself had placed over creation's fullness. Over these thorns he encountered the downside of a culture formed by genera-tions of thinking and responses to fallen reality. The term I will use for this 'downside' belief system of a culture is 'generational strongholds'. From there he faced the power structures that had formed in response to the culture and its strongholds. Finally, in the atmospheres over these power structures, he came up against the angelic forces of the second heaven. Any sphere of creation, any culture we as sons and daughters desire to engage, occupy and thus fill will present to us the same array of challenge. Hence the importance of gaining a clear sense of the divine strategy of overthrow as exemplified in the life of Jesus.

Before we proceed, let's look at a graphic to help us better visualise the journey Jesus took.

The journey through creation

Principalities and powers

Power structures

Generational strongholds

Thorns

Third heaven

As with Jesus, our forerunner, the first thing we face in our journey towards the heavens are the thorns. These thorns are given by God to help reveal to us the state of our heart; that we might know what needs to be overcome to get through to our inheritance in creation. This God-designed way of communication is multi-layered, with each layer representing a level of engagement that brings us closer to the fullness. Again, these levels or layers we need to overcome are personal strongholds (revealed by the thorns), generational strongholds (inherent or fixed in the culture that surrounds us), power structures (controlling institutions over people and process that come into being via their manipulation or use of generational strongholds) and principalities and powers (angels of the second heaven that enforce and garrison the works of fallen humankind and the power structures these give rise to on earth).

The thorns over creation's fullness tend, one might say, to accumulate lots of human activity and thus attract a good deal of angelic attention because they mark the borders at which futility begins (Rom. 8:20). It's a bit like traffic stopped by an obstacle, queuing up and waiting to get through to its destination. It is because these thorns are the place where the action is concentrated that Satan uses them as a primary base for his plan to have dominion. The process whereby undue power accumulates over the thorns is not that difficult to explain. Over many generations, as people come up against the futility of life, they will seek to gain the sense of security and significance they lack in undue ways. They will grasp for power and dominate others, seek the security of being ruled by another, turn to the idol for strength rather than to God for truth, and so on. Thus, at the point of creation futility, they will find themselves, to one degree or another, either ruling or being ruled. Whichever position they take, they will find themselves dominated by strongholds raised up against the knowledge of God and thus manipulated by fallen powers over their sphere or principality. Thus, the composite of fallen reality, the same that is established over every sphere of creation we desire and are called to engage, is formed. I note here in passing that the same process happens in regard to establishing the good and going for the fullness.

It was into this 'state' of things that Jesus came. It was through this state of things that Jesus had to blaze salvation's trail. He was born to travel right into the heart of Israel, there to pierce the core of its power structures. Only through this work could he dislodge the power of angels and make a way through the second heaven to the third over earth. To put it another way, Samaritans did not kill Jesus on his way to Galilee. The Pharisees crucified him with help from the Romans. What Jesus did, in effect, was go into Israel and draw out the powers of man and angels to move against and kill him. It was in this act of murder that these power structures surrendered their judicial rights to authority in Israel and thereby lost their hold over the good and divine things that had been under their jurisdiction. It is essential that we see the strategic suffering and death Jesus went through in the light of its impact on the power structures on earth and the powers of the angels of the second heaven. Again, it is that way of salvation that we are created and called to follow. Are we ready and willing to follow him?

Heroes of death, life and faith

Christ is of course the instigator of the most dramatic transition that has ever taken place in human history. There are many other examples we can draw from in Scriptures that are in line with the spirit and intent of his work. These many accounts of transition from old to new indicate that the times we find ourselves in are not exceptional. Let's take a look at one such account, the struggle of Elijah against the reign of Ahab and Jezebel. It's a helpful account because it contains many parallels to what has happened in the church in the West over the past five to ten years.

We know the story well – the kingdom of Ahab and Jezebel and their sin; the drought and the increasing desperation this judgement brought to Israel; the call to Elijah to return from exile and his meeting with Ahab. From there we read of the confrontation on Mount Carmel and the severe blow divinely dealt to the influence and power of the prophets of Baal. After the fire descended the rain broke over the land, Elijah ran before the chariot of Ahab. And then . . . Jezebel got scared and ran home to Phoenicia.

Ahab got sorry and invited Elijah to be his mentor. The remaining prophets of Baal resigned and got day jobs baking bread ... not quite. Instead, Jezebel, enraged, moved to kill Elijah and he, traumatised, both by post-revival-let-down syndrome and that uneasy feeling that comes with a monarch's displeasure, ran away to the desert, where he told God that it would be best if he killed him before Jezebel did. Some wafers and water later Elijah was told to anoint a new king and a new prophet. It was only after these things were done that he was allowed to take his fiery chariot ride to the third heaven.

It is interesting to track Elijah's journey with the past few years of the church's experience. We have had a season of rain in the body of Christ that has brought refreshing to our souls and freed us in many ways from the growing constraint and limitation that we had been experiencing. I am, of course, aware that not all streams of the church experienced the same and that much of the movement I am now referring to happened in more charismatic/evangelical and Pentecostal settings. Again, we need to see the body as one body. Thus what has happened (in what is now the second largest facet of the church on earth) tells a great deal; even in those places that differ and did not cover the same territory as the above streams in recent years. The anticipation in this renewal was that the rain of blessing would usher in a time of revival, which would cause those outside the kingdom to come flooding in to the church culture and construct. This would vindicate the local church's place in the divine plan and answer the saints' desire to impact the earth for God. Many good things did of course happen, but the reality is that none of the above-mentioned things did.

The question is asked: Where did the drought in the time of Elijah come from? Was it imposed because God was judging the nations around Israel? No. This drought came as a result of the kingdom of Israel going wrong. It arose because Israel was operating on the basis of an ungodly and illegitimate mandate – one that Jezebel helped to fix in place and Ahab submitted to. Drawing a parallel between this judgement and our present experience, I would assert that the drought we as the church experienced at the end of the 1980s and into the early 1990s, the drought that the rains of refreshing came to break, had little to do with the world system or the devil and most to do with the way the church itself was structured. Thus the rains that came were not for the validation of the present set-up; rather they came to prepare a way for its ultimate overthrow and the emergence of the new.

As mentioned, it was soon after the revival let-down that the corporate styled church (that which had come to prominence during the 1980s) in particular took the new tag apostle to itself and used it to reassert its authority over God's people in a much stronger manner than before. As this was happening the disappointment from revival let-down caused many to reassess, like never before, their relationship to the church as construct. The move of the Holy Spirit in renewal had freed up many of the saints and they found that the ground under their feet was now more moist and supple than before. Into this ground many began to plant the seed of their good desire for work, life and inheritance. Also many church leaders were no longer as confident in their role as they were five/ten years ago. Many from that time on have begun to look more carefully, even sceptically, at the promises made at the height of the conferences they now attend.

An emphasis on one person's authority over the people and the process is now on the rise and many are seeing its nature more clearly than they have before. Will it be the moist ground under our feet or a man as monarch over and above us? These options are now set in far stronger contrast before us. We, like Elijah of old, find ourselves entering, after the rain, into a decisive and direct confrontation with the very stronghold, the very power structures that have held the kingdom down for centuries. Hence the need to look anew, in the light of Hebrew vision, at the strategy of engagement and overthrow employed by Jesus during his time on earth.

Chapter 12

Troublemaker by Birth

At Jesus' dedication in the Temple the divine process of overthrow of the powers that had held the people in bondage for generations was prophesied by Simeon. He declared: 'Behold, this child is appointed for the fall and rise of many in Israel, and for a sign to be opposed and a sword will pierce even your (Mary's) own soul – to the end that thoughts from many hearts may be revealed' (Lk. 2:34–5). Whenever God does a new thing, the effect of it will be the same. It will reveal hearts, be opposed and ultimately call forth a divinely ordained death, a death that breaks open a new way for the saints towards the fullness.

I have mentioned the increasing move by saints into the new landscape. Even though many in the present church construct look on this with suspicion and concern, I believe it is a move ordained by God in line with his purposes. The new creation seed now growing in the life of many saints is causing them to take hold of a greater freedom to live their life and do their works. For these people the church as construct is no longer their main place or point of reference for life and work. Many times I have asked the following question of people who would be considered by their pastors to be highly committed to the things of God and the things of church. I ask them how much space their church takes up in their thinking and planning. The general answer comes back at around 3 to 5 per cent. This contrasts with the situation in prior years where the answer would have been more like 20 per cent.

One church leader I spoke to said it well. Twenty years ago we, as leaders, would say to the people that we are going here and doing this and they would, for the greater part, follow us wholeheartedly. These people have now grown up, got a job, a family, a mortgage and identify with various networks of people. So now when we tell them that we are going here and doing this they give us some money and tell us to go and do it. The leader said to me that if this attitude continued he knew he was looking over the next three to five years at the demise of what he had known to be church. The question for this church leader is what should he do in relation to this growing drift beyond his local church into the 'out there'? Would he get with it and lose the power base he had established, or resist it and lose a good deal of credibility, and indeed integrity, built up over many years of telling the people they were the church and preparing them to get into life for God. They were finally taking him seriously and he was nervous about where it all might lead.

As was the case with Jesus growing up in Nazareth, the new move initially presents little challenge to the power structures. However over time, as the momentum increases, those in power will find themselves challenged and stirred to respond one way or the other. As things continue it will be very hard for any leader to remain neutral. Many will, of course, try and corral the new move by having a two-pronged approach – church here and market-place ministry there. However, the same old kingdom divided scenario will no longer hold the water of the now rising tide. The difference between the current move and past innovations in ministry is that it is not happening in and from the local church culture. Most developments in church over the past fifty or so years relate to ways leaders can build better and bigger congregations. Many leaders have become accustomed to, shall we say, a rather controlled release of the saints because of this. Not many have, as yet, dared to contemplate a fulsome release beyond the church as construct into creation. Their doctrine of the church has to date not permitted them to countenance such an eventuality.

Thus, the new emerging, as was the case with the appearing of Christ in Israel, is a challenge to the way things are, a test to the platonic 'state' of things. Those in authority over the church as construct, be they leaders or power-brokers, are experiencing a challenge to their way of leadership, the likes of which they have not known before. Their response to the new emergence is coming under the divine spotlight. The 'thoughts and intents' of their heart are being brought out into the light of a day of judgement. As with the work of Christ, a work that took place mostly away from the synagogues and the temple, the new seed growing beyond the congregation is not heading away from the power structures. Rather it is heading straight into the very heart of the church as construct. It moves in this direction because its life and creative freedom challenges the status quo. The new move is hitting at the heart of the authority of those accustomed to occupying the centre of the church construct. It is stirring up those who to date have been in charge of most of the kingdom initiatives and the resources that fuel them. This good work of the new creation church is designed to travel into the domain of the platonic agenda, there to draw out into the open its nature, its heart and its intent. Again, when you begin to create from your heart and move towards the new you are not walking away from the old; rather, you are walking right into and through it to the inheritance it holds. It thus stands to reason that over time opposition to what you are being and doing will arise. It is not an accident; it is a critical part of the divine strategy for overthrow.

The heart of the matter

Jesus, via his works and his words, took that same journey into the heart of Israel. Within that heart were the promises, the covenants, the fathers and the purpose that had to enter into the soon coming new covenant. As he moved with the Father and ministered he necessarily came up against the generational strongholds resident in the power structures of the Pharisees, Sadducees and Roman overlords. This was tolerated for a season, but over time, as a momentum for the new began to develop, opposition from those who loved power became inevitable. Jesus was drawing out these power structures to reveal their heart and ultimately bring them into destruction. It is through that judgement and the death it brings that the release of the good within the old is affected.

One fellow I spoke with from the UK was amazed at the extent to which certain church leaders in the city, known for their capacity for innovation in ministry and for being on the cutting edge of what the Spirit was doing, had, in a short space of time, become so fixated on who was on their 'team' and who was not. They began to stress loyalty to the leader and to the vision and demanded that this fellow decide if he was going to pursue his own personal ministry or the church's ministry to the city. If he chose not to follow the church then he was to step away from the fellowship. Friends of this fellow were also being asked to choose which initiative and thus which set of relationships they were going to give themselves to. This happened in a local church that had never apparently been occupied with the loyalty thing.

Leaders, like every other person, do not know their heart until it is challenged.

As the move by saints into the new continues and increases those who stand as one with the power structures will begin to move to protect their rights to the people and process. This is seen in the reaction of the Pharisees to Jesus. As they witnessed the growing response of the people towards him, they began to publicly challenge him by questioning his motives and interpreting his sayings to make it look like he was a pretender or a heretic. The old will always resist the new for what it sees as very good reasons. 'We need to care for the people, because without our leadership they will scatter.' 'We need to be good stewards of the kingdom and thus keep organising and directing the activities and resources of the saints.' 'We need to be very careful that people just don't do their own thing because a spirit of individuality makes people selfish.' And on the list might go; all of them apparently good reasons to do controlling things so as not to lose one's hold over the centre. These justifications, made with increasing intensity in response to the new, begin to give away the real intent of those in power. Their stiffening of resistance to the new and the shoring up of their own authority base causes people looking on to begin to consider the issues relating to individual freedom and authority like never before. People like Nicodemus looked at the life and works of Jesus as contrasted with the talk and deeds of the Pharisees and decided to pay him a visit and ask him about the nature of his power and the source of his freedom.

Logs and specks

The reaction of people to the new will not always be done from evil or wrong motives. Many will move with genuine concern and theological back-up to question the new. Often this questioning and the unsettling of the status quo that causes it are the first steps in a journey of change for those in leadership. That being said, it needs to be noted that history is replete with people who did evil things for what they saw at the time were good and godly motives. As Jesus said, there will come a time when the people who kill you will think they are doing the will of God. Again, the matter is complex. Here we are endeavouring to follow a particular vein of response to the new; this to highlight the move by the power structures ruled by fallen angels to maintain their control over the systems of humankind.

In line with this it is also important to look at the base from which the reaction to the new emerges. In some settings it will be from the church leader, but in other instances the power base might be the elders, the deacons or say, in one instance I am aware of, the family that has been in charge of the church organ for three generations. Again it is important that we do not just assume that our pastor is always the main perpetrator of crimes against humanity. The stronghold is in our midst and, as such, is shared by all of us to one degree or another. As good work from good desire starts to gain momentum and draws the powers out into the open then, generally, a specific faction will take the sword and move on behalf of the status quo against the new. There are many instances in local churches where the first casualty of transition is the minister.

Whilst stopping for breath and some qualifications let's also look at some concerns that might arise at this point. Some might question what is being said here, saying things like: 'what about those who are evil and need to be judged and excluded from fellowship? Surely we have the right and the responsibility to move against them? Are you saying we should no longer speak against that which we disagree with? What if the people pressing for the new are deceiving themselves and in fact pushing to take control? If everyone just said and did what was right in their eyes, then the outcome will be pandemonium. Surely this is not appropriate?' These questions could go on and on and serve to indicate why this book is not a manual about how to get there, giving fifty steps along the way with set responses to each challenge and situation. Rather, we are looking here at a description that only puts in place an outline of the process. It is our thinking and relating in response to the many issues this season of change brings that are at the heart of the matter. This matter before us is not simple. It will not respond easily to standard people management techniques and easy evaluations of others' motives by those in authority.

It is very easy for those heading into the new to mistake reaction for creativity. Both bring a sense of freedom to the heart, but it is only through the good work that the new can emerge. Expectations that are built up over years and end in disappointment bring hurt and anger that fuel reaction against the church construct; particularly if those in authority begin to criticise your actions and question your motives as you move out to create. During Christ's life he was strong and honest when speaking about the power structures, but always affirmed the divine value of what they held within their jurisdiction. The platonic agenda at the centre of the construct will often move those in its power to oppose you, this with a view to getting you running from and reacting against the church. If you do, you in effect step away from the attributes, nature and power of God these structures presently hold within their jurisdiction. The power structure at the centre is well protected by counsels that come your way with a view to picking a fight it knows you cannot win if you react. If it cannot keep you under its jurisdiction it will then move to drive you out. If it can do this via your reaction and anger it can then declare you a renegade, not worthy of any person's consideration. So when the pressure mounts and the criticism comes, explain yourself as best you can, stay in place as much as is possible and keep creating. Don't do this for the express purposes of showing the powers that be how free you are. Do it because your good desire and heart to engage creation and please the Father leads you to do so.

Crunch time

As more people respond to the new the power structure will come to the same place reached by the Pharisees of old. A state of play was reached in Jesus' ministry that caused one of their numbers to say, 'If we let him go on like this, all men will believe in him, and the Romans will come and take away both our place and our nation' (Jn. 11:48). It is here that a critical turning point is reached. The powers of the centre now know that they are under threat. The number of people now reaching for and moving into the new is creating too many holes in the dam wall. The state of things is now such that something must be done to plug the breaks, lest the place and station of those in authority is lost. At this point in the divine strategy the decision is made to move against the new in a more overt and hostile way. In effect the decision is made to destroy it. It is in this killing that the overthrow of the old is assured and the emergence of the new is guaranteed. One cannot say just when this will occur in the transition. It has a lot to do with the stage the new has reached, with decisions made both by those in the new landscape and by those in positions of authority. Ultimately of course it has to do with the timing of God in the matter. We read in Matthew 26:3, 4, 'Then the chief priests and the elders of the people were gathered together in the court of the high priest, named Caiaphas; and they plotted together to seize Jesus by stealth, and kill him.'

Our Western society does not permit churches to execute the wayward. In the present age, however, there are many ways to kill. The main way is to simply dislodge the person from the life of the community. You can take away their position of influence, rendering them persona non grata. You can engage in character assassination that cuts off their rights to a fair trial. In every case the intent is the same, to eradicate the influence of that which threatens the status quo. This decision to move against and kill the new may not happen in every instance. Those in authority might well decide to give way to the new. To do this however, there will still need to be a dying process. The strongholds that have held the particular construct in place will not leave simply because the pastor has decided to change tack. When any church minister decides to take a hold of the new they will still need to do battle with the platonic agenda. The extent of this battle will depend on how much of the structure they have built has been formed by idealism and other expressions of the platonic leaven. Some leaders will have much to pay if they are to die to the church contract they have inherited and/or established. Some will have less. However, we, as leaders, must all face some write-off in the face of death if we are to see change come to our own lives and to the lives of those we hope to see released into the new. It is important to be reminded here that leaders of the current church construct do not necessarily have the control that their job descriptions indicate. We will look in more detail at the leaders' response in this regard in chapter 14.

Two-way death

Jesus' journey through the thorns, his travail into the heart of Israel, took him into the jaws of the powers that be and to death. It was essential that the Son of God come this far and go through at this point. For, as mentioned, it is in this place of his divine dying that the power structures are exposed and pierced at the heart and thus their overthrow assured. The killing of that which is of God by those who act as one with the power structures as well as the divine dying of those seeking to pursue the new have profound consequences. When the old moves to kill those who embody what is emerging, it is in effect killing that which is new within itself. It once believed in freedom, but not this kind of freedom. It once believed in releasing the body into creation, but not this kind of release. It once prepared for a harvest that would fill the building, but cannot countenance a move that happens outside of its jurisdiction.

When the old moves to kill the new it, in effect, surrenders its right to partake of the new. In fact, it is killing any and all of that which is new within it. Its inability to affirm facets of the new, for fear that it will be mistaken by others as a vindication of it, keep it from speaking in support of, or travelling down, that new way. Many who could not clearly see the new are, as the old moves against it, now able to do so. They recognise in the killing of the new that there is more arising in them that identifies with the new than the construct of the old. They begin to distance themselves personally from the old and seek after the new with greater fervency. Thus the death of martyrs became the seed of the church.

When someone becomes murderous and justifies their action on the basis of their authority to do so, it causes them to accelerate into that downward spiral to death. To substantiate one's unjust actions one has to keep revisiting those actions, repeating them with double the gusto to prove to oneself and others that they were valid. Once you try and get more meaning out of that which flies in the face of life, you draw down more darkness and thus become increasingly submerged in it. Such is the way of divine judgement, in that it hands the individual over to that which he wants, with the punishment and consequence inherent in that hand over. Saul's right to be king in Israel was taken from him because of his disobedience and rejection of God's purposes. Over time he increasingly moved to kill anyone who threatened his power base. In particular he had it in for someone who, more than anyone else, represented the new over the old – that being David, the son of Jesse. Saul finally fell on his own sword, his death making a way for the new in David to lay hold of the divine purpose and kingdom resource.

At this time of being killed we need to be careful not to rise up and react against those in the system moving against us. It is one thing to resist the temptation to burn against those who burn against you. It is another thing to sit by and let someone kill you. When you are killed you are free, but if you kill you are ever bound to that which you have murdered. If we rise up and kill the old, using the same tactics used by it against us, then we will not be able to carry that which is good in the old into our lives in the new. If David had followed through with the wishes of his fellow soldiers and killed Saul in the cave, then he would have carried the same murderous spirit into the new. He would have lost much of the good that was held within the kingdom construct. Even when Saul fell on his sword, David did not gloat or rejoice in his demise. Rather, he moved to extol the greatness of the man and his reign, thus aligning his spirit and drawing into his life the best, rather than the worst, of what had been. We see an unsuccessful journey through transition evidenced in the life of Oliver Cromwell. He moved against the old in a militant way and over time became murderous (Ireland) and thereby failed to carry what was in his heart/passion into a new era. In the end Britain rejected him and much of what might have been new was lost.

Those who are killed are now free to take the best of that which has been with them into the new season. They are free to lay hold of the attributes, nature and power in the heritage and wells of their forefathers and go through to the land that is calling their name. The old has surrendered its rights to the goods and these are now given to those who have moved from death to life. They are now free to take the life in those goods and use those goods for more of life. As we shall see, to make it this far in the divine journey these saints will have of necessity seen many strongholds within their minds brought down. This again is a critical part of the divine strategy of overthrow. We will track more of the individual's journey in this transition in the following chapter.

What does a local church construct look like after this time of judgement? I don't know. I would say however that it will no longer be able to hold power over people from its centre as it once did. I do know that this process of transition from construct to creation will not be ideal or clean. It will be messy and muddy, as was the life, suffering, death and resurrection of Jesus. As the judgement makes its way through the house of God, the responses of many will be a surprise. Those we felt would never change will die to the old and embrace the new. Those whom we felt were free from the love of position will hold on for dear life. Essentially it's not a matter of what this one or that one does however. It's more a matter of what we ourselves will do when the heat is on.

The old may well control what it thinks is the centre of the church process for years to come, but its death and the life of the new is assured as this way of judgement travels to its culmination. Ahab and Jezebel continued on for some years, thinking they had the right to others' vineyards and fields. During this time Ahab was blessed and won victories in war. However, his days as king, along with his alliance with Jezebel, were numbered.

When I survey

This way of suffering our way into the new is not an obscure teaching of Scripture. Rather it stands as central to the strategy of the kingdom's coming. Yes, Jesus died on the cross for our sins, but also by his death he went through to secure freedom from strongholds that gave the principalities and powers their rights over us. When he rose from the dead and ascended he took the power and rights of the cross, and by them 'disarmed the rulers and authorities' (Col. 2:15). We need to look anew at the death he endured that he might pierce the heart of the powers that ruled; at the price he paid to disarm the angelic principalities that backed up these earthly powers; and, finally, at the joy he felt as he journeyed through, disarmed the powers and took his place in the third of the heavens over earth. In the same way Paul became one who filled up that which is lacking in the afflictions of Christ, suffering his way into the very heart of cities and lancing the boil of their generational strongholds. In this way David (in relation to Saul), Elijah (in relation to Jezebel), Moses (in relation to Pharaoh), and Jeremiah (in relation to the false prophets, priests and rulers of his day) each took this journey of suffering and death; a journey that liberated them as it served to liberate a people and a nation.

When Jesus said that the strong man was bound, was it only via the works of healing, or was it in line with Colossians – the triumph is in the cross? The strong man who holds the goods is only bound when he no longer has power to rule the hearts and minds of people. Yes, the miraculous is a part of the sign that will stir and demonstrate to people that the new is arising. However, the system that held Israel's inheritance (goods) was not won by the miraculous. It was not exposed by the miraculous and it was definitely not brought to its knees by the miraculous. It was exposed and undone when it killed the prince of life. It was exposed and undone when it moved against the greatest good that had ever walked the planet. It surrendered its right when it wrongfully used its power to destroy the one who created all things. There is no more final a defeat of platonic inspired control and power than this – in this way it is killed judicially under justice, culturally by those who desert it to identify with the new, thoroughly by the death of all that was good in itself and completely by its embracing of death itself in the killing of the new.

If we are looking for real change as his body the church, it is not more leadership and better programmes we need. Rather we need to go into divine death. Only then will the age-old serpent be answered and the body of Christ rendered free of platonic infection; set free to move with good desire to search out and gather to itself the good attributes, nature and power in all things. This journey is one that is taken individually as well as together. We now turn to focus specifically on the individual journey, a journey that takes one past one's own strongholds through the thorns of life, there to gather the full inheritance into one's heart.

Chapter 13

The Journey Through

When we decide to move into the new, we commence a journey that will take us right into the domain inhabited by power structures. There we come up against, not so much the enemy, as that which is in and of us. As mentioned, the journey of the individual in this time of transition is not something separate to the power structure. These structures are formed from generations of thinking, deciding and doing. Thus, to disregard, react against or destroy them is to deny a reality that is an essential part of who we are. God gave us thorns that would tell us more about ourselves than almost any other thing on earth. As mentioned, around those thorns he allowed the generational strongholds to form power structures. These structures are now integral to the thorns we need to go through to gain our inheritance. They are as much a sign of our reality as were the initial thorns placed over certain bushes on the first day after the Fall. They are, in effect, those same thorns grown large in every creation sphere over many generations. Scary, I know, but let us embrace their invitation to what is real.

When we are moved by good desire to go into the good work we are moving towards the reality of our creation inheritance. As we come up against the power structures and the generational strongholds they contain, the resistance we meet becomes our teacher. It performs a service that enables us to measure where we stand in relation to our inheritance in creation. It is therefore important to know and feel the weight of power structures coming against us as we head into the new. This is God's given way to help us know where we are in the process of transition from old to new. They help us pace our journey through the thorns and into the goods presently held by the strong man over the domain we are challenging.

In truth, if we did not come up against this resistance we would have so much open space before us that we would not know the direction in which to travail. It is not advisable to dream that all obstacles be removed and all structures destroyed to make a way for your aspirations to fly. If the dream came true, which it won't, it would only leave you in the rubble, confused about who you were and where you were. You would in fact be unable to build anything new. Instead, you would end up repeating the old; either by your reaction or because of the human tendency to repeat cycles of dysfunctional behaviour that have not been properly sorted out.

As in the days of old God 'will not drive them [your enemies] out before you in a single year, that the land may not become desolate, and the beasts of the field become too numerous for you' (Ex. 23:29). Instead he will 'drive them out before you little by little, until you become fruitful and take possession of the land' (Ex. 23:29–30). Each parcel of land holds its own power, history and underlying creation challenge that needs to be known and travailed through if the inheritance therein is to be released to the sons and daughters. Let's start with that underlying creation inheritance.

Correspondence from creation

When the saint moves in line with good desire and seeks to create in the new they will, as mentioned, feel resistance. This will generally commence in the mind of the saint a long time before there is an obvious reaction of the status quo against them. The reason for this is that the very creation space they are seeking to occupy will begin to 'correspond' with them in relation to what needs to be subdued before they can enter in and settle that particular ground. Remember that before the Fall and the thorns came in the creation held the good, the resource, the substance. They awaited the arrival of the image bearers, to yield its fullness over time to them. As it is with any good love of one for another, that love is not easily given away. It waits to sense the trust, enjoy the pursuit, know the soul and only then release the heart. This holding back creates the tension that connects one heart to the other. The bond this creates between them is thereby made all that much stronger when the choice is made to yield.

As this cry, this invitation to occupy comes back from the particular creation sphere it will begin to draw out the good desire of the heart and the personal fears surrounding the individual's strongholds. This helps the individual locate the ground they want to occupy and locate their heart desire for that ground. In this awareness they will feel the nature and extent of the challenge before them, begin to get a taste for the attributes, nature and power in that ground and, as mentioned, start to touch the strongholds that need to be overcome if they are to enter in and occupy.

It is important that you locate the creation ground you want to occupy and feel the weight of its challenge before you do business with the strong man in residence in the power structure over that ground. This ensures that it is your desire for the good, rather than any reaction against the old, which is at the head of the procession into the new. If you are led by reaction, you are led away from and not towards your inheritance in the land. The clearest vision one can have through the thorns and all that surround them is a line of sight gifted by good desire. This heart desire, breathed into and through by the divine, enables us to go through, come what may. We cannot long be motivated by a passion to overthrow the status quo. If we are then we will either end up locked in a room with six other reactionaries, or become the next demagogue of the latest version of the old. We were made to create, not react. The powers will move against you, but they will ultimately have a no show in that battle if they find a heart moved to create by good desire.

Trip wire

As saints move further down the track of their good desire they will necessarily begin to activate the counsels that protect the strongholds that hold the power structures in place. These counsels are things such as reasons or assertions that justify and protect the position held by the power structure. We see this way of response in the life of Jesus as the Pharisees, threatened by his words and deeds, began to rally their interpretations of tradition and Scriptures to oppose him. It's important that we realise how finely tuned these counsels are, how precise their aim and effective their capacity to hit our own personal set of strongholds. They are well armed to guard against anything or anyone that tries to oppose the status quo they protect. They have been honed by generations of use, constructed to play on the fears of a thousand hearts. They are designed to play on people's desire for significance and security, for meaning and love, for reality and for God, for power, for control and comfort. They are well equipped to strike their blows against the mind of those seeking to break out of the status quo and inhabit the new.

The counsels that protect the generational strongholds of the power structures come in many shapes and sizes. For the most part they are verbal and take the form of an implied or overt threat to your need of security and significance. 'If you don't comply you will be out of here.' 'Everybody thinks this way. How dare you say that years of good people's work are wrong.' 'Who are you to think you are right?' 'You are out of order, a threat that must be taken out of the way.' 'You are on your own now, at sea with no strong parameters or minders to define or guarantee the outcome.' 'There's no money in this, no one is going to buy it.' 'You'll be deemed a fool for stepping out into no man's land.' 'That you are a fake and don't really know what you are talking about will soon be made more than obvious to everyone.' You could no doubt add to this list statements, threats and accusations that you have heard (or have found yourself saying) in times past. As they move against you they activate the counsels of fear that cover and defend the underlying strongholds in your mind. It is in this way they are used by God to draw out what you really think and believe about yourself.

As these slings and arrows come against us and activate our own strongholds we, in a word, experience pain – emotional, cognitive and at times physical. We feel uncertainty, fear of rejection, loneliness, drivenness to perform, despair and other thinking emotions commensurate with the particular stronghold being triggered. In essence we begin to know and feel the suffering spoken of in Romans 8:17. Again, this emotional and cognitive pain is not our enemy. It is the gift of God, creation's greatest reality sign for your life; one we need to embrace and follow if we are to know what holds us back from our inheritance. It is this pain that Jesus wants to transform into a travail that can guide the process of birth into the new. Such a perspective enables us to understand how power structures can be transformed from an adversary to an unwilling ally in the dance of change.

As we continue to press in to the new, our correspondence with creation and the stirring up of the power structure against us increases. This causes our fellowship with Christ's suffering to also intensify – bone from marrow, spirit from soul, the time-sands within are sifted to make way for the gold of the good to emerge. As our fellowship with Christ's suffering deepens, what is true and of good desire within begin to travail. Our pain is now strongly pushing the eternal promise towards the life eternal. I covered this part of the journey in some detail in chapter 9 of *The Church Beyond the Congregation*. Briefly here, the Son of God, through his incarnation, came to fill every facet of human experience. He made his way through every judgement that arose from the Fall. He went through the suffering, the thorns, the death and into eternal life. As such, he now occupies the place of our pain and suffering. He is there to transform it into a travail that can take us through to life and inheritance. This is the reason why we read in Romans 8:17 that 'we are heirs of the Father and joint heirs of the Son, if indeed we suffer with him'. Unless our strongholds are activated by reality, unless we feel the pain of that activation, unless we follow the journey that pain takes us into healing, we will not be able to come into our full inheritance in creation.

It is in this place of intense correspondence with creation and the earthly and angelic powers that we come to know our heart like never before. 'I feel the need to be secure but the new does not offer such security. In fact the more I press into the new the more insecure I feel.' 'In my dreams

I am a pioneer, but in reality I crave for someone to take charge and occupy central stage.' 'I decided to get out there and create something new. Now a few months into it my leaders have gone quiet and I am not getting the support I need.' 'When I am with the crowd I feel so strong, I can do anything. Now I am doing something myself I fear I will not succeed; if the truth were known I feel helpless and hopeless.' 'I moved to initiate and they did not appreciate the importance of what I was doing. I'll show them, I'll prove to them who I am, just wait and see what I am going to bring to pass.' As the process of transition continues these inner struggles meet with the external struggle to bring things to a head.

Twelve-step programme

We have looked at the pain that comes from our correspondence with creation and the opposition of the powers. It is important here to also mention the pain that comes simply from the lack and/or loss of what we had in the old. Perhaps the best way to communicate this is to compare it to a person's rehabilitation from addiction. Almost all of our lives we have been programmed by platonic idealism to be dependent on a centre that we think holds the key to life. We have become addicted to the substance called the ideal and made to think that only in association with the leader, the anointed, the vision, the knowledge will we be able to experience success and arrival. Even for those who have given up waiting for the construct to deliver, there is still a residual lift that they get week by week by their association with it. To move away from this and to begin to place your life in creation at the centre of the divine purpose is to enter a process of rehabilitation occasioned by times of strong pain and deep loss.

To move from dependence on a central construct to follow one's good desire of heart in creation takes time. We have not been well trained to trust this desire. Nor have we been taught to see our eternal inheritance in our life and work in the spheres of creation. When we move from the ideal construct and engage more decidedly in our work in creation, the first time period will, generally, feel good. After a time, however, we will necessarily begin to crave for the patterning and affirmation of the old. Leaders are like father figures, as such, when we are no longer under their direction we can feel a loss of security and identity. The present church construct, having taken jurisdiction over the gathering, the Spirit, Word and Law, the ministry gifts and the name church, ensures that if one breaks from its ranks one will have to leave quite a lot behind. It needs to be said that I am not referring necessarily to a person leaving fellowship and not responding to leadership in any shape or form. More so, when a person begins to change within, when their desires for life and inheritance are stirred towards creation, they will sense a distancing from the way things were before.

Even if your leaders are supportive you will still feel the pain created by the distance that is now between yourself and them. In many cases this affirmation will mostly only be verbal; this because most church leaders are presently still too busy looking after meetings in the household to become one with the church as fullness. However, even if leaders do join the journey into creation, your relationship with them will be on a very different basis to what it was before. Like a child grown and leaving home to make a life, you will and must feel the trauma of leaving. Certainly you will, or may, come back to have dinner every other week, but things will never be the same again.

For many moving into their life and work in creation the situation back at the church as construct will not be as releasing. For years to come these saints will arrive in the gathering and find the leader still talking about the destiny of his church, the ministries commenced and those planned for this year. They will keep calling for volunteers and money. The songs will commence and the sermon will follow, but the heart will not be able to agree and unite as in times past with the sound they make. This pain of separation will of necessity cause guilt and alienation in the life of the person stirred to enter into the new. Hence the need to know the nature and redemptive purpose of the suffering these bring.

The situation is complex and we are only passing through here. However, we need to track this part of the process of travail to bring these emotions into the dying of Jesus. The experience described above is a great opportunity for death to come to strongholds and a corresponding freedom from addiction to arise in our life. People speak of depression and loss of a sense of purpose during such times. One fellow said that for years and years he had followed the church programme and when that was no longer deemed to be his Christian centre he found himself all at sea. The leaders of his fellowship were active in releasing the centre and creating a culture that could serve the new. Even though this was the case, he still had to go through the change in his own life. For many months he sat at home with his wife night after night. He attended some church meetings but was no longer able, as was the case in the past, to grasp them as his primary meaning base for Christian life. He confessed to watching too much TV during that time (honest fellow).

There they sat, the husband with remote control and the wife trying to concentrate on one programme as he flicked backwards and forwards for months on end. Every so often they would turn off the tube, look at each other and wonder what it was they now wanted. Several years on this fellow has completed his MA in health promotion and is a major link person between agencies in this area of the state's health care services. His wife has had their first child and is now expecting a second. Things like this can happen when you turn off the television. This is not to say that this would not have happened, or cannot happen, in present church set-ups. What made the difference in my observation was that when they became the church primary rather than the church secondary, when the meetings were no longer central and primary in defining their Christian life, they were able to focus more clearly and decide more strongly in relation to the things that made for their life in creation. These folk are now much more decidedly being and building the church as fullness in the creation spheres of marriage and work, but it took time for them to locate a heart that had for years been trained to look first to the church as construct. The disorientation they felt when they first found themselves at sea was the beginning of a process that taught their heart to swim the oceans of God's good earth.

Dying time

As the heat from the powers that be travels up the scale, the fellowship with Christ's suffering move into the time Scripture describes as being 'conformed to his death' (Phil. 3:10). The threats of the power structures are, for the most part, real. They do hold many of the resources, power, affirmation and people within their jurisdiction. Hence when they begin to move to 'put you out' (Jn. 9:34) they, generally, will have the ability to do so. In effect, these power structures can kill you. It is in this killing and through this death that the powers are overthrown in one's life and the goods they hold are released to resource the occupation of the new ground. Before we rush ahead to grasp this victory, we need to look anew at death that God has so perfectly designed to set us free. It was God who allowed death to come in after the Fall. It was God who came to fill that death in the incarnation, taking away its sting and making it the doorway to life. That same death, the dead-end and full stop embedded behind the thorns, has now been broken through and the way into the fullness, the inheritance, the life eternal made again. The question is, will we go the way of this divine death? The words sound nice on paper, but in reality we would much rather this cup pass from us and any other way through than this be found.

Again, the fullness is through the thorns, which are surrounded by power structures, which themselves are formed by generational strongholds; these strongholds are protected by counsels and the fallen angels back up these power structures. When the Son of God came he went through all of this, not to eradicate it and thus remove its capacity to reveal what is real, but so he could make a way and show us that way. He wanted us to come into confrontation with what is real inside ourselves. He did not come to pluck us from reality so that we could then hop over the thorns and skip to a spiritual heaven in the next life. He came to give us life, not fantasy.

Death for Jesus was, of course, the most difficult experience of his life on earth. The greatest temptation he faced was to choose not to die for our sake. When Peter turned to him and said, 'You shall surely not die', the response by Jesus was made directly to the devil in the words 'get behind me Satan'. The struggle continued right through to the time in Gethsemane, but thankfully he died and made a way through. Now we must die or there will be no way through. It is the fear of death that will keep us in bondage all of our life (Heb. 2:15). When we no longer fear death we are free, free to engage the pain and let it show us how to travail the child of promise to life. If we half take this journey, pretending to move out but all the time holding on to the old, we will only prolong the death God has ordained for our freedom. I hasten to add here, to guard against certain consciences' capacity for self-accusation, that none of us will take the journey perfectly. We will all have to pretend to be braver than we really are, taking one step at a time, looking for grace to decide, die and live as each new day sends its good and evil stuff our way.

Shattered strongholds

The power structures and the angelic powers that back them up know what you are going after. They know that they are not simply losing your allegiance to their centre; but that you are moving closer to the 'goods' they hold under their jurisdiction. This is why they ultimately will move against you to cut you off and kill you. We have covered this part of the journey into the new in terms of the larger picture. The journey for the individual is the same. The larger picture can only take shape and form up as a critical mass of saints move into the new landscape to gain the goods necessary to occupy. The individual cannot precipitate the overthrow of overriding power structures. Their freedom from inordinate power comes when their own strongholds die the death; this assisted by the move of power structures to kill them. When an individual is 'killed' the jurisdiction of the particular power structure over them is broken and the attributes, nature and power it holds is then released into that person's life.

In time, as mentioned, as those with freedom breathe that good in prophecy and prayer over others, then more people will be able to choose to journey through into the new. As this happens the larger overthrow scenario will follow the course set by the more individually oriented journey. This kind of progression is seen in the way Paul, at the end of Ephesians, taught the saints to pray first for one another as the church and then several years later in 1 Timothy directed the same kind of prayer towards those in positions of power over an entire city. I briefly add here that by using the term 'individually oriented' I am not referring to a lone journey. This path is, yes, one that you will travel in many ways alone, with your heart and that of God your Father. However, it will also be a journey taken with one, two or more others, connected as his body, fitted and held together by generous servings of truth and love. I do not want to give the impression that this journey is a lone ranger affair. Rather, I am making a distinction between the journey of the individual in relation to the overriding power structure and that which relates to a larger people movement in the new, which signals a stronger cultural or societal overthrow of the old.

When the powers move to kill you, there is a final opportunity given you to resist, react, run and return to safe ground. However, if you keep creating – don't try to die, that is something that only Jesus can enact for and in you – then you will find that the blow that cuts you off will be the blow that sets you free. That blow, those words, that dismissal, that character assassination will work to shatter your now highly exposed strongholds. At this time you have no other option but to let go of these strongholds. If you hold onto them your pain will be unbearable. For even though the powers think they are moving to kill you, they are in effect moving to kill your attachment and identification with generational strongholds. Remember they don't have the power of life; they only have the power with regard to the lie.

Just as Satan moved to kill the prince of life, thinking that such would complete his programme of evil, the powers are stirred and driven to move against us. As was the case with Christ, it in that move the powers find, not the victory they had gleefully anticipated, but rather their own defeat. During this time of 'killing' the blows that come upon our strongholds put such pressure on them that we can no longer ally with them. The good desires these strongholds have masked and distorted are now appearing and the lie can no longer suppress the life and truth that is in them. In this divine dying you will feel yourself coming apart, you acutely feel the sense of loss and pain as this happens. The dissolution of ways of thinking that have so strongly defined your life and made you ripe to be ruled by another are complete in this death. It is here that strongholds die their death and you find your life. God takes up the sword of the power structure, uses it to deliver the saint from internal bondage and when the process is complete causes the structure to fall on that same sword. Only God could do such a thing!

Barney and Paul

A friend, call him Barney, who had been in local church ministry for over twenty years on the pastoral staff, had been introducing many new initiatives with a view to releasing the saints into life and seeing congregations in the city come into closer relationships. This was applauded for many years. However the time came when the release became, shall we say, too releasing. This caused some of the business people in leadership in the church to get into the ear of the senior pastor. They said that it was time to take stock of resources and thus better steward the church. So, under pressure and uncertain of his own standing in the matter, the pastor agreed to pay for a business audit. It was designed to work out where the money was going and the extent to which that money was serving the vision of the local church. As such it began to cut against much of what Barney had been creating. He challenged the leadership to consider that they were no longer releasing people and resources to bless the life and work of the entire body of Christ in the city. By this time, however, the more corporate model for church life had taken hold of the centre. Barney, his work and position now effectively killed, made the decision to move on. He now is free to take those many years of good work into his present work to network the emerging church on the landscape.

Another fellow, call him Paul, commenced a very effective ministry, one reasonably well known throughout his nation. It was, when it appeared, quite a cultural innovation and enriched many who over the years identified with it. There came a time when Paul realised that what had started as a grass roots move was now becoming too centred on him. It had also become too much of a product producing institution. So, he decided to lessen the authority of the centre and begin to spread the work into autonomous groups with the desire to take these on. Initially many welcomed the space he created, but over time many in leadership began to get nervous. They felt they would lose what God had entrusted to them over the years. So, they moved to shore up the centre. To do so, they had to move, first politely and then firmly, against Paul. In effect, Paul was killed and is no longer with that movement. He is, however, now free (although hurt) to pursue what is in his heart for the new and, as he said, is now more released from the need to control than ever before. His prophetic sight has grown and more and more leaders of movements are coming to him to learn about the death he died and the life-space he now occupies.

I am not saying that Barney and Paul performed perfectly in and through all of this. They no doubt got too angry at times. They might have had moments of arrogance and self-pity and yes, even over reaction. Thank goodness, for this gives us all hope that we too can go through. For a long time they still felt the pain and hurt of being killed by those they loved and worked with. However, the more they saw into the nature and purpose of the death they died and located the divine moment therein, the more their wounds stop bleeding life's blood. A scar still remains to remind them of the price they paid for freedom – not just freedom from power structures, but also freedom from the thinking within that binds.

Life after death

After your death you will remain for a time in the dust of its dying, fellowshipping with Jesus in that zero moment from which one learns to count afresh. And as you emerge from death you will find new sight to locate your freedom from the old. You will find within and without a greater capacity to create, work and relate because you no longer have to fight that constant mind battle against the banal or sophisticated array of counsels that used to hold you down and harass you. You now have judicial permission to carry the best of the old into the new season. When you speak and build you find that the Nicolaitan spirit can no longer mess around with what you do. Yes, the propensities of the old strongholds will of course still reside in the sin nature and at any time we can still choose to respond. However, our mind is no longer as framed and as formed by them. The enemy will come but will find his hook can no longer attach to fallen flesh animated by idealism. In leadership positions you might occupy you will find that authority does not settle on you like it used to. It will no longer draw people to some centre, causing the anointing, the power and the truth to stick to you and your ministry or organisation like it once did. Rather we will see the power of the Word spoken come to settle, as God intended, on the people and their work. This is a great freedom indeed, a freedom that will cause a new loyalty to spring up between saints themselves rather than between people and ideal constructs.

If we move back or sideways in response to this pain to some safe or prior place then the generational stronghold in the power structure has won the day – and so it should. For if we do not change by embracing the dying of Jesus, and thus the out-resurrection life that follows it, then we will not have the capacity to actually occupy the new ground. We often think that we have occupied because we have prayed it, sung it, heard it, confessed and dreamed it. However, it is only when we live it by working it that we in reality engage the substance of it in creation. This is why there is so much written in the Scriptures, particularly in the New Testament, about the nature and purpose of work. It is only in our work that all of the elements of truth, choice, desire, relationship, testing and more intersect in reality. Many of these things can be mimicked in a meeting, rehearsed in a dream, performed on our behalf by a leader, but it is only as our life journeys towards the fullness in and through our own work that we are able to really engage and answer the cry of a waiting creation.

There is no use pretending we are going to occupy the earth if we are psychologically dependent on something or someone other to keep telling us who we are, where we belong and what we should do. Yes, stronger patterning is appropriate for the initial years of Christian life, but these early years are only a preparation for creation. They were never to be used to train a person for life centred on a building or a cell. If we cannot get past our own addiction to the ideal, then there is no use pretending we have any-thing to offer the planet in terms of a way of life and a way to God. It is far better that we know the place we really occupy and the platonic substances we are presently addicted to. We can no longer continually echo songs and sermons of bravado off the back wall of our church constructs thinking that such will impress men and angels. Thank God his divine reality is coming down on our ideal subculture, squeezing us out into the creation reality and crushing that which is not real in the process.

Travelling light

At this time many are being stirred to create and take the journey. It is good for each one to consider the cost, count the bricks and then decide to pace the journey with Christ into death. The providence of this time is colliding to create a time of large-scale change in the nature of things. God is moving, as in the days of Elijah, in judgement on the house of God. This needs to happen firstly throughout his body the church, if we are to see it happen in health, business, education, government, the arts and so on. This is why the judgement begins in the places that the sons and daughters are most strongly identified with. The saints can and will emerge from this time of judgement substantially free of ideological centres and ideologues. They will no longer be easy pickings for the next new fad promising arrival. Their addiction to something else, something other, something ideal will be over and they will learn the life that feels what is true. They will learn to feel pain rather than suppress it. They will learn to work life in creation rather than mostly rehearse it in meetings. They will learn to discern love that is real and relational and ignore that which is ideal and not real.

As we live such a life and do the works that occupy then the powers over principalities, already disarmed by the resurrection of Christ, will give way for righteous angels to come and stand in line with our life and work as saints. It is only as we journey through our own personal strongholds, those that hold us back from the true knowledge of God, that we can move past the counsels of generational strongholds and bust the powers of these controlling structures. Only then will the 'manifold wisdom of God be made known through the church to the rulers and the authorities in the heavenly places'. As this wisdom is established on earth then those guardians of the created order, those angelic second-heaven mediators and counterparts between the realm of man and the throne of God will move to back up, intensify and garrison the creation reality we have established. Only then will our work be established in the atmospheres over earth, giving the souls waiting in darkness the breath and the creation waiting in hope the love that calls forth. In this way, and only in this way, can we as his body the church grow through the second heavens of these angelic hosts towards the fullness that sounds the sound of our soon and coming arrival in the third. The dying of Jesus is now before us as his body, the church; will we accept his divine invitation to life?

Chapter 14

Leaders in Transition

I was tempted to name this chapter 'Leaders – When to Breathe, When to Push'; this is in line with the different stages of the birth process, particularly in relation to what is called the transition phase of the process. Giving birth has always been a great motif and reality sign of the divine process. The most amazing and redemptive sign God gave after the Fall, one that was written strong in the judgements designed to bring reality to bear on the decision Adam and Eve made, was the sign of pain in birth. Scripture says that the whole of creation groans in travail to see its fullness come to birth. Among the many amazing things about birth is that the woman, for the most part, is regulated in what she does by a kind of pure pain. Most of the time she seems to have little control. Pain takes her on a journey she cannot fathom, rationalise or, as mentioned, control. The whole process is geared to the child of that birth, the pain given to move that child into life. It is in and through that most amazing of events that the girl emerges as a woman, and the woman emerges as a mother. We may never give birth ourselves, particularly if we are men! However, this primal journey of letting go and trusting pain to bring us life is one we must all take time and again.

Scripture informs us that leaders have a double dose of opportunity, responsibility and thus judgement in their backpack. This means that when it is time to give birth, they will feel a double dose of birth pangs. They will need to doubly give way and trust the pain to bring them and others they relate to into life. As mentioned, much of what has happened in the past few decades in regard to church strategy has been about pastors building bigger and better congregations. To my mind this has produced much dysfunction in the ranks of the saints. They have gown accustomed to church being for the most part about them, having to do primarily with things like the size and comfort of their sanctuary and the wit and anointing of their preacher.

This has meant that much of the price that pastors have had to pay to date has arisen from having to keep up with the demands created by consumer-programmed saints. If leaders perform to market specifications, supplying their people with a strong centre and a vision tipping towards transcendence, giving them regular doses of idealism, making them think that the cutting edge is never far away and that revival, or at least congregation growth, is just around the corner, then, as one pastor friend confided in me, they will be able to keep ahead of the pack and keep them coming. This sharp prod into our present consumption-obsessed version of church is, again, somewhat of an exaggeration. That being said, I wish it were further from the truth than it is. We have been so trained and regulated by consumerism in regard to our way of church life that much of our theology and practice has become rationalised and woven into a way of leadership that is kept dancing to its tune.

It is against this backdrop, or perhaps I should say, it is poised over this cliff edge, that the following is posited. I have painted it thus to give us a sense of what we are up against, of what God is at work to judge, to remind our hearts of why we need real change, to urge on our good desire for a new birth to come. As leaders we have quite some responsibility in the matter before us. Often the arguments leaders use to ensure that things remain the same (whilst appearing to change on the surface) tend to draw attention to the more positive aspects of what is basically a very dysfunctional situation and argue that to radically change the status quo would be to somehow deny or take away the good things built up over many years. This capacity for rationalisation, theological and other, makes it necessary to more starkly bring to mind the underlying dysfunction of our present church construct. We need to remind ourselves, as we make decisions concerning the future course of the church, of its platonic foundations, its consumer-driven idealism and of the extent of stagnation these have brought to Christ's body, the church.

The judgement now on the house will, to my mind, ensure that it will mostly be our pain that teaches and thus leads us. Many leaders are now in a place where they have tried it all. Decades of doing this and that in an attempt to fill creation via their construct have faltered. They now turn up on Sunday to face those same faces looking back at them, demanding answers that seem to have run out the door. The spirit and wells of salvation, those things we signed up for all those years ago, still live within our heart and each of those faces. The waters of the eternal are breaking. We will not be able to control what comes, we can only, and we must, trust our pain like never before. We must keep breathing till the time is right and the Spirit alongside, the Paraclete of midwifery, tells us to push. The divine pain will intensify and burn before the child as yet unnamed is born. From girl to woman to mother, from boy to man to father, we will then look back, child in arms, to see what God has done. First, though, the pangs of birth.

Pain management

I have spoken of the way in which leaders of the church as construct become more and more identified with that construct and of how, over time, they, one might say, 'morph' across to become one with it. Some are better at maintaining a distance, but this is more often something achieved mostly in relation to themselves. Their congregation still identifies them first and foremost with the centre of the church process. Many pastors cannot or do not maintain that personal distance. They may start out that way but over time are carried by market demands to a place where they become one with the seat of power from which ecclesiastic deliveries are made. Many pastors I have spoken to tell of the feeling of being imprisoned inside their church, unable to escape, locked inside their ministerial persona. Other pastors rejoice in this submersion of their person into the role of pastor and priest, they make full use of it to generate a following and build their base.

It follows from this then that when the judgement begins on the house, the persona of the pastor, identified as it is with the church as construct, comes under much more divine pressure than the person in the pew. When divine fire begins to light on the roof of the collapsing house and the rafters get that infernal look about them, ministers are often the first to feel the heat. It's a hard place and a hard call, but how can we, as leaders, expect the rest of the saints to go through the dying and into life if we are too scared to do it ourselves? This double judgement is a part of our employment package. Another thing that follows from pastors' oneness with the church as construct is that it gives them a capacity (and responsibility) to encourage an environment that welcomes rather than resists the divine initiative. They can actively work to establish a setting for divine judgement to more easily, or cleanly (with less undue destruction for the people) break the platonic hold at the centre of the construct.

The reminder of the sign of birth hopefully will help us not to believe that we, as leaders, can actually bring about this change. We cannot socially engineer the death of the old and the emergence of the new in the same managerial and didactic way that we have to date been accustomed to. That being said, because most saints are identified with the church as construct and have little or no knowledge of the church as fullness, our role as leaders is very important. The convictions, motivations and knowledge that work to form our way of leadership during this time of transition are, as one might well imagine, critical. These will be tried and tested at this time of judgement like never before. As mentioned, most of the innovations in church concern better ways to build bigger congregations. However, uniquely, this time of judgement and transition has little to do with that kind of outcome. Yes, one would anticipate greater growth over time arising from the release of the body into the spheres of creation. However this growth may never return to your building, and it will never come back under the same authority regime it has been under in times past.

This move is about the life of the body, not the preservation of a movement or a meeting. This is why the judgement on the house works so strongly to reveal the thoughts and intents of every heart. The assurance we have is that the more we, the church, engage and answer the cry of creation the greater will be the response and abundance of life that will return into our lap. However, unless we are willing to give it away, we will never see that richness return to our lap. So, what kind of things can those in leadership positions do to assist the judgement and transition process?

The lines of sight to follow are in no way prescriptive. There is not a ten-point method, or step-by-step programme sold at a corner stall for leaders in need of a quick fix. The tendency towards such an approach, one that over many decades we have been trained to expect, is one of the reasons why I approach this chapter with some degree of reticence. One more point before we proceed: Do try to keep in your mind as you read what follows that everything that we have come to appreciate about the church – the gathering, the word, the presence of God, the worship and more – we are wanting to carry with us into the new. What we are looking at here is a process whereby the way that they are presently (platonically) configured can be taken apart so that they can be free to be more, not less, of what God wants them to be. Let's begin with an account from a pastor in the throes of divine dying.

I spoke with a group of pastors about this dying process and, during the discussion, one leader let out a gasp. He said that's it, that's what's happening. The church I pastor has been dying for months now. Whenever I prayed about it, I felt to let it go. For so many years I had been trained to rally the troops, get a new vision, scold the wayward back into line. But now my sense was just to leave it and see where things would take us. As soon as I did this I felt so guilty. Like letting a child die or something. However, I didn't have the energy and could no longer muster the passion. I felt like a really bad leader for letting things slide, but I could no longer raise the flag and get people to muster and salute around it. This has been happening for a number of months now and a few families have left saying that the place is not functioning properly, but again I am not going to rescue it. I know all the leadership stuff and I know I could steady the ark for a few more years, but I also know that we will come round once again, at an even older age, to the same old question – what are we doing here each Sunday?

I asked him what life he had seen emerge of late. It took a few moments, pained as he was by the extent of dying, and then he said: The young people seem to be going really well. They have seen some of their friends saved and are really enjoying the freedom to create and grow that the fellowship now offers. They come to me when they need advice and I do keep an eye on things, but they just seem to be getting on with life. Yes, also, a few new families have joined and they are appreciating the sense of community and honesty in the place. It's strange, these new people and new Christians don't seem to be noticing all the death that's going on. They just seem to think it's great. I shake my head and wonder what will I have left at the end of all this.

Removalist ministry

If I had to succinctly summarise what a leader might do in this time of transition, I would say: Do all you can to carefully and decidedly remove 'the centre' from your culture and practice of church. I would hope that this statement would, in line with the ground we have covered, be reasonably self-evident. The centre that holds together the church as construct, the one established by platonic idealism, oriented towards the removed transcendent realm, made separate to the life of the saints, the one that commandeers the name and resources of church must be carried into death. We as leaders cannot ourselves kill it. This is because its reality is based on generations of thinking found both in us and in those around us. Indeed, if we move to too quickly appear to kill it by, say, closing down the whole show and walking away, we will find that most all of the people, including ourselves, will remain unchanged. It is only through a divine dying of individual strongholds that separation via death to generational strongholds and the powers that rule because of them will be affected – hence, the need to focus clearly on our purpose here.

It is as we move to take away the centre (psychological, spiritual, authoritative, managerial) that a change will be effected in the relationship of the saints (and ourselves as leaders) to our way of being church. This process will draw out strongholds in people and will also draw out, in line with the process we have looked at in prior chapters, the powers that sit at the centre of the church as construct. As those in leadership work towards the removal of the centre, the divine process of overthrow and transition will be assisted and accelerated. How then might one carefully and decidedly remove the centre that has been in place for over sixteen centuries – the initial answer is, with great difficulty! Thank God that he is in, through and over it all or we would just be rearranging the furniture. Much of what follows is reasonably simple, and many will already be doing the things suggested. Again, it is not so much this or that thing that we might do; it is the intent and understanding we have as we proceed that matters. Hence a call to not take the form and lose the content, to know why we are releasing resources, naming rights, elements that make for church and ultimately people from the central construct and what we are dismantling as we do.

As per normal leadership principles, one would hope that the leader is in good relationship with a core group who are deemed to be in oversight. There needs to be a conversation and a level of agreement here concerning the state of things in the church and the need for transition before it moves out into the larger congregation. The reasoning for this is obvious: new things take better shape in small groups, which then expand – the example of Jesus and the twelve disciples indicate this – 120 people, then

500 and then a multitude come to believe (or rise against the Christ and crucify him!). The conversation concerning change and transition has been happening in many settings for some years now. Many have been engaged in innovation regarding more fluid expressions of the church. In Great Britain the exploration of the Celtic Christian heritage, a form of church that was much more open (as distinct from the Roman centrist church that came in during the fourth century) has set a strong foundation in place for a more creation engaging way of being the church to emerge. Eastern Orthodoxy has a spirituality that is also more life-oriented than the culture of church derived from the Enlightenment. As such many have searched down that line for greater sight. In the past few years, the Hebrew vision of creation and the doctrine of church that arises from it have been well received by many. These and other resources are now on the table and can help stimulate our conversation together with regard to transition.

I don't want to spend time looking at the way this conversation might go, because one cannot really say. Some leaders will find out sooner rather than later that they are going to be killed. Other leaders will discover that their leadership position was not as secure as they had imagined a month before this conversation commenced. Some will be surprised to find that many of their friends, protagonists and even their adversaries on the leadership team have been thinking along these lines for the past few years, but did not dare proclaim their heresy for fear of the guillotine. The progress of such a group discussion, either in terms of a growing affirmation or a growing fear of the new (or a mixture of both) will be a good litmus test for what things might look like down the track in the larger congregational setting. This conversation sets in place a level and power of agreement for the time ahead.

Not one centre but two

A good way to start to subvert the centre is to start another one and have them both operating at the same time. This will confuse fallen angels and righteous deacons like nothing else! Positioning yourself outside the church as construct sends a message to the home crew that you, as a leader, deem this to also be a place where you as a minister should be found. As you spend more time with people in relation to their work, particularly with those who are not in 'your' congregation, and less time taking care of church business you begin to pattern a new way. This patterning can begin to have its effect a long time before you launch into a preaching series on radical change. These series on their own will, as we know, come and go in six weeks and generally leave the congregation much the same. People are moved by what we do more than by what we say. For years they have heard sermons that speak of being on the verge of radical change, and nothing has changed. We need to forgive them if they are not moved by the promises in our preaching anymore. As people begin to realise that the minister now has two or more centres of focus and he names each one as church, then there is an opportunity afforded the congregation to experience that first flush of divine confusion on its countenance. They could even be forgiven for thinking that things are in fact changing.

You could begin by regularly visiting the owner or manager of a small or medium business and discuss the issues they face. Enjoy being a novice and learn from them. It will be your desire to better understand and share in the hard reality of what goes on in the world of work that will be as much an encouragement as any of the wisdom and revelation you might offer to them. In time you might begin to, for example, help build the team in that business and create a more redemptive and productive environment in which the saints and others can thrive. Try not to jump into this role too quickly. Spend a number of months listening before you consider such a move. Let those in the world of work ask you to step up to this level of involvement. Let them know of your interest, but don't invite yourself too soon into the process. This way of relationship gives the saints the necessary permission and agreement they need to begin to be and build the church as fullness in their settings. It also trains the ministry gift to stand and equip these saints, in line with Ephesians 4:11–16, more directly for the work of ministry they are involved in. You might ask how can we do this when we have a church of hundreds? What about all the other business people and those in health, education, those unemployed or factory workers, won't I be neglecting them? The answer is that we are not trying to manage the process; we are simply setting out on a new course and need to begin, as Jesus did, with one or two initially.

When you create more than one centre you, in effect, draw a line between the two points and are then able to begin to fill the space in between. Our relationship with those in the world of work can teach us as much, if not more, as those we minister to. I do not want to go into more detail about the relationship between ministry gift and the saint in the new, such is for another time, suffice to say that the encouragement and richness we gain from serving the saints in this way will quickly give one a taste for life as a ministry gift to the church as fullness.

As you draw from the well of the saints' work you can then begin to showcase this work and its importance in the gathering. In most churches the conversation is about the church, its mission, its needs and its leadership. The self-centred focus needs to change for a shift to come. As you begin to draw out and showcase different parables (examples) from the life and work of the saints in the spheres of creation you set a better context in which you can begin to teach and demonstrate more about the new. In the light of these living examples, words about being the church in all of life and work will begin to make more sense. Often those from the leadership team who have been able to engage in a longer and stronger discussion concerning the new, those working in the world of work that have travelled some distance down the track can, in particular, be brought forward as parables to good effect.

As these parables and pioneers come to the fore, you can begin to rename things. In different gatherings and settings call these people and what they do 'church'. Deem their work to be at the forefront of the kingdom and tell people that the gathering is subservient to it. Tell people it's not about the vision of the church as an organisation; it's about each person's heart desire. It's not about meetings and programmes and departments the church sets up for you; it's about the good work and initiatives in the home, the place of work and the community. Again, as we do this then people might just dare begin to believe that change is in the air. Use these opportunities, as Tony Campolo said, to change the price tags. Do not try and sell the change by over idealising it. This is to play into the hands of an old sales technique. If we overstate the case by making things appear more than they really are, we will create an expectation that can't be met. Much of the disappointment we now face in the present construct of church comes from making the good things God was saying appear more than they were in reality, thereby blowing them out of the water. Speak well of these parables, but don't overdo it.

Stated policy of underperformance

Resource allocation is a big issue in our churches, run as
they are like small businesses. When the pastor begins to
do things that are outside the camp, in particular things
that do not enhance the prestige of the church, then people
will begin to wonder where their money is going. This
sounds a little harsh and in many instances social etiquette
will ensure that the initial response to the pastor not being
available in the office as he used to be will be more subtle
and muted. A recent survey in the USA said that most money
donated to church is used up in the internal programme of
the church to service the needs of the parishioners. Not
only is this giving on the way down, but also the external
giving outside of the church to outreach programmes,
missions and the poor had fallen to a thirty-year low. When
a pastor, who is meant to be working for the church, begins
to work with others outside, then all of a sudden the amount
that the church does for its people begins to lessen. To my
mind this lessening of delivery is a must if we are to begin
to wean people from what has become a very dysfunctional
and consumer-fixated arrangement.

As a leader, you have been trained and are expected to
fill in almost all of the gaps in church life with your presence,
your words and your activity. In our own situation, a few
months after the decision was made to dismantle the centre
and gaps began to occur, certain people began to fear that
what had been would be no longer. It was like a panic
buying thing set in. All of a sudden there was a call for
more prayer, more Bible study and more cells. My response
was to encourage people to do these things if they felt they
should, but that we would not name them as church proper
over and against the person working in the home or
business. This lack of church naming caused those who

had wanted more prayer meetings to lose much of their resolve in the matter. If it was not church, then it was just prayer, like prayer in any other setting. They had been accustomed to 'the centre' delivering and giving meaning and authority to church activities for many years. Now that there was a level playing field everyone had the right, in relationship to others and the elders, to be church. The situation became indistinct and more fluid than it had ever been because the definition of what was and was not church was blurring.

In one setting I know of, the departmental structuring of the church was gradually dismantled. The pastor's reasoning to the congregation was there should not exist a department for anything that should be a value in one's life. People should do pastoral care, evangelism, prayer and so on, but not 'be' departments on others' behalf. Such, he said, engenders dependence on the construct and immaturity and laziness on the part of the people. As the pastoral care department was removed, people feared that the church would no longer be able to care for people. How would care be organised? Who would you bring people to see? Some began to rise up against this move and declare that there was no longer enough love and care for hurting people. The reality was that the same pastoral care was still being done, but it was no longer considered to be the church doing it. It did not have the church name attached to it. The pastors were overseeing and ensured that no one fell through the gaps. Over time people, feeling the need and concerned about the lack of care, began to occupy that space and take greater initiative than ever before. This outcome was not accomplished by leadership from the front. It happened as the leader stopped leading and left space for decisions to be made and things to be done.

The response to what we no longer do will precipitate change in a far greater way than that which we say or do.

People are accustomed to things being added, it is a strange thing indeed when a service they have been accustomed to getting from their leaders is withdrawn. It is time that we, as leaders, stop dancing to the impossible demand we have created and decide to underperform our way back to reality. As we begin to draw back from this life of supply-side ministry, we are inviting a strange feeling of space to invade our local church setting. This space is a dangerous, unknown and alien space. It sends a fear into the heart of the powers that be and signals to righteous angels that things are definitely opening up. This space is something that God is able to make very good use of in regard to his programme of judgement, death and life.

On reading the above one might think it to be a recipe for disaster. There are so many churches now advertising their ability to meet need and supply answers and resource. The fear here is that if you do not compete by offering the same or better then you are dead in the water. Again, our conviction as leaders in the matter will be tested. If you head out with an army not large enough in commitment to overcome, then terms of peace need to be sought. If the congregation is your source in life, and you do not want to act in such a way as to threaten that source, then it is best that you don't underperform. If you pretend to go into this death, you are of all ministers most to be pitied. In most every instance where deep and lasting change has happened in corporate and/or church settings, the individual has been committed to losing it all in the attempt to win the prize. It sounds like a familiar principle, does it not?

The truth is that the extent and nature of the judgement coming down on the house means that to attempt to perform to market expectation is going to become harder and harder over the years to come. Many presently have some store of good will and good wine in their church cellar.

Is it not best as a leader to rewrite your contract with those around you now because in five years time you may find yourself with very little to bargain with? The crowd and market forces have never been a good indicator of what we, as ministry gifts of Christ, should do. It's time we measured leadership and success in a very different way. Again, our conviction and faith, drawn out into the open by much of that pure pain, will be strongly tried during this time of travail. If we have little or no faith in regard to this change process, if our faith resides in the size of our Sunday attendance and our Sunday offering, then it is best that we discover that sooner rather than later and do business with God accordingly.

Fragmenting within and without

Remember that our intention is to dismantle the central construct that has to date been identified as church. As we separate the things that have fuelled that centre and place them elsewhere, fragmentation in the church construct and the mind of the saints will begin. The name church and the ministry gifts now operate inside and outside of the building. The works of ministry now include cleaning an office building or driving a bus. The home becomes as important a place of being church as the Sunday meeting. As these things become integral to the culture of church then the primacy and prestige of the mother ship will begin its descent to earth. We need to actively work in such a way that the sense of centre in the mind of the saint begins to come apart. This may sound like manipulation, but it is no different from the process currently used to bring all of these elements together so that they form as one construct in the mind of the saints. It is not the process we use, it is the intent and outcome of that process that makes a critical difference when settling the issue of manipulation.

It is during this time of more evident coming apart that the strongholds in the minds of people (and those of leaders) will begin to stir and find their voice. Many who have thought that to pursue the church as fullness idea, or to go Celtic was the way to go, now find that their safe Sunday haven from the storm of life is no longer as safe as it was. Again, people mostly respond to what happens around them, not what is said. Even the showcases of parables in the new landscape and stories of impact will be taken by an old mindset and used to shore up that sense that 'our church' is going somewhere. It is only when 'our church' no longer tries to go anywhere, as a construct that is, that most people will sit up, start taking notes and then begin, with the real them now activated, to enter the fray and have their say. This progression follows the strategy pursued by Christ. He worked to draw the heart of individuals and powers out into the open. Remember, the purpose is to see the thoughts and intents deeply hidden in people, and the counsels kept safe inside the belly of the construct, rise up for good and ill to face the reality of divine judgement.

Leaders need to breathe faith at this time. This, of course, will not make the pain go away, but it will help. It is at this time that more intense questions about the transition will be asked. These questions, fuelled by real pain and a sense of loss, need to be met with an answer that springs from faith. Rather than being cagey about the now faltering state of things church, leaders can inform people about the strategic importance of the sense of loss they are feeling. They can point to the reality of dependence and the possibility of maturity this time of change affords. They can say to those who did not expect a real baby to arrive, those now startled in the throes of an unanticipated birth, to breathe! That is, they can go with the pain and let it be a

guide, rather than go against or muffle it. It is at this time
that the powers of the church as construct are being strongly
shaken. The generational strongholds are no longer being
obeyed. The fallen angels are no longer getting their due.
As we maintain our stand as leaders – remember we are
still gathering, still talking, still praying and worshipping –
then righteous angels gather and heaven stands in ever-
stronger agreement with us. The divine space we have
helped to create is now easing apart the tangled platonic
centre. The Gordian knot is being unravelled. The powers
within the construct are being exposed. The hearts of many,
along with our own hearts as leaders, are being revealed
like never before.

Thanks for what you have done and, by the way, I'm angry

One local church decided that their transformation would
be helped if they no longer met weekly on a Sunday, but
instead gathered in homes, meeting once a month in a larger
celebration event. The culture that the leadership sought to
breathe into and through this was not the classic cell model
of church. They certainly employed elements of it, but
further to this they sought to de-emphasise the small
meeting as being central and to place and build the people's
sense of community and being of church across different
networks in their city. I attended a meeting of the small
group facilitators about four months after the shift in
emphasis and structure had occurred. The things said during
that meeting are very indicative of the course that transition
takes in the human heart.

To a person these leaders felt both a sense of loss at
what had been taken away and a sense of newfound opportunity before them as saints. One person said that he never

really enjoyed the worship service, but liked coming each Sunday and seeing all the people. The other day he said, I began, for the first time in a long time, to want to worship. So, I put on a worship CD and praised God for hours. I surprised myself. I am not sure if I like what you have done to my Sunday meeting and my old version of church, but I have to admit that the space I now have is making me have to decide what I want. Another person said that having Sunday free and not being able to do much caused them to feel somewhat at sea for a while. A few weeks back, he said, we decided to invite the neighbours over and we had a great time connecting. We enjoyed it so much that we have decided to make Sundays a day to invite new people over. The fellow also said that he was uncertain if he could trust what the leaders had done in taking away their church, but did admit that the space was being enjoyed by his children and their in-laws and gradually giving opportunity for them to connect with people in a way that they had not done for years. One fellow was somewhat angry, but at the same time appreciative. He said all of my life I have been institutionalised (he was an orphan) and even when I became a Christian I now realise that I was further institutionalised. Now for the first time in my life I have to decide about what I am to do with my discretionary time. I have to make a choice. That is so hard, but I know it's doing me good.

The pastors of the fellowship were debriefing later on and some felt that they should spend more time trying to alleviate the pain of those going through the change. As we spoke on this the resolve was that, although it was good to keep up the encouragement, the pain was actually the very thing that was causing real change to happen. It is a tendency in the pastoral care culture of the present church set-up to step in too quickly and alleviate tension and pain and fill the space with guarantees of future resolution and, in this and other ways, to give overmuch comfort. These people were now experiencing pain as their strongholds of dependence went into the dying of Jesus. This death was being, as it were, overseen and, as such, assisted by those in eldership.

In this process of dying the leaders were not exempt or distant. They acutely felt the pain, anger and disappointment of those who have to date depended on them to deliver the church thing. It is as they kept in place that sense of space and unresolved tension that their own dying to a way of living and leadership took place inside of them. As this happens the leadership dynamic changes, the control and management tendencies, well honed by years of use, begin to fragment and fade. Again, the platonic centre is found more in the circle of leadership than it is in the space inhabited by the congregation. It was amazing, in the above setting, to see the way in which the removal of the church centre brought people's strongholds to the fore and how these strongholds were being dealt with in the very space created by that removal. There is a third stage in the birth process. It happens when the pain and the midwife tell you that you can strop concentrating on the breathing thing; you can now push. At this stage you are both more out of control but have more power in relation to the birth than ever. It's time to take heart in the words of the Father – 'Shall I bring to the point of birth, and not give delivery?' (Is. 66:9).

Chapter 15

Birth Comes to a Head

In line with the process we have tracked in prior chapters, there comes a time when things will reach a critical phase. It is at this time when the particular fellowship reaches a point where the balances are about to tip towards the new, so much so that the old will be no more. As much as people intellectually and emotionally might fathom the changes, even the most deconstructed saint will still need to experience a more decisive time of dying to the old – even if this has most to do with feeling it alongside others going through it. It is at this time that the culture in general (one might say the critical mass of people in the group) decides to either commit to the new or fight for the old. Some, of course, will simply leave the fellowship to find something like the old they have lost. Those in leadership who are assisting the process of change will encounter, to one degree or another, a time when the change will be challenged like never before because the powers, earthly and angelic, are losing their hold over a people and a process. It is a critical time, a time when the Nicolaitan stronghold is making its loudest noise. The very life of the platonic virus is now threatened.

At this stage, counsellors in the fellowship might launch an offensive related to the quality and extent of pastoral care, the business heads might launch a takeover in the name of good stewardship, or perhaps the sure and steady elders might reach out to save what they see as the now faltering ark. In these instances those who decide and have the power to do so can kill the pastor. Again, if this happens the pastor is free, judicially to enter the new. In many instances, however, this critical phase can be ridden through. When this time is reached there is often quite a sense of death in the atmosphere. Those in your leadership team, the ones who were 100 per cent behind change, may have dropped back to less than 50 per cent by now. They might be telling you on a regular basis that they are uncertain if anything might be left at the end of this madcap exercise. Attendance and giving might be down. That being said, attendance might be up – one cannot say – but generally things won't be like they once were. It is an amazing time in the life of a group of people, a time for courage and wisdom from leadership.

By way of autobiography, the two years that I went through it with around one hundred people were some of the most amazing and testing of my ministerial life. I, and those around me, changed so much during that time. There were many surprises regarding who handled it and moved through, and who could not cope and spun out. Many who did not cope and decided to leave the fellowship returned a few years later to thank me for being the first leader they had who had really challenged them to grow. They had gone to other more centrist fellowships and had not been able to sense the reality there that they had begun to feel in the setting they had left. Even though they no longer attended our set of meetings or associated closely with us relationally, the seed of the new had been planted and drawn out sufficiently to commence a process that came to fruition after they had left.

I cannot say how this death will finally happen, in that it can happen a thousand different ways or it can appear to happen and in fact not be happening at all. It may be wrong of me to suggest that we should look for a more defining time of decisive change. I suppose, because in our own situation there was a marked time of change, I tend that way. It can of course happen through a series of deaths, whereby the old gives way to the new. It could happen, I imagine, more gradually without there being a need for such measurable and distinct events. The times of transition in Scripture do seem to be marked by definitive events. However, even there the cultural change arising from say Elijah's dealings with Jezebel, or Jesus with the power system in Israel, did not become evident until some time had elapsed. Again, it's the principles and reality that relate to the overthrow of the platonic centre that are in view here, more than this method or that description of events.

When shove comes to push

There comes that time when people know that the way that their church life has been defined and structured is no longer going to be. Moves to shore it up, pressure to fix it and attempts to restore what has been lost have not been successful. The leadership have kept standing with others in their conviction to see the centre removed and no pressure has been able to change that stance. Generally there will be, as mentioned, some attempt to rescue the situation. As this rescue is mounted, in whatever form it might take, those in leadership should not react or kill in response to the onslaught. Instead, allow the death that such a move against the new accelerates to have its way. During this time your reputation as a leader or as a church might be verbally killed, your motives questioned, your history exaggerated – whatever, it all amounts to a death in you and via that a further and final death to the platonic agenda now falling on its sword. As with most good spiritual warfare, keep relating, smiling, feeling the pain – in all, keep standing. You are in a good place, a divine place, a blessed place. You are now well into the dying of Jesus. It's time to start pushing.

In our own setting it was the attachment to a way of church that certain people had known for decades that became the main motivation for those who tried to keep the old going against all odds. I was going to include a more detailed description of the set of events that precipitated the death, but it would perhaps have lent too much weight to a particular version of the end game. Suffice to say that there came a time when some in the leadership team decided to resign their position and move on. This precipitated a strong backlash against myself and was used to garrison the position of those fighting for the old. Again, I stood. It's not always best to pretend one is like Martin Luther, but in reality I had gone so far into this, that I 'could do no other'. It was a strong blow to a now frail situation. For me it hit against a set of personal counsels that had been to date hidden in me, bringing them to the surface for divine review and death. I don't want to give the impression that this move accomplished the death; rather, it helped precipitate the final stages of it. The straw that broke . . . and all that.

We thought that the Sunday following this would be a hard fought and heavy one. The time came and we arrived, set up the sound system and waited for the somewhat tired and depleted group to arrive. Our network was still strong and many identified with us, but the struggle of the past few months of more evident death and the option given to people to search out and decide concerning how they might best express their Christian life had taken its toll in terms of numbers. In preparation for our joining with a Methodist congregation we had also moved venues and met on Sundays an hour earlier. That morning, however, to our surprise when we commenced and moved to worship we began to realise that something had changed. One prophet had declared several months back that there would come a time when the meeting would be over and the gathering would begin. That morning that is exactly what we experienced.

We breathed an atmosphere so different from the heaviness of the past few months. There was no longer any centre we had to maypole around. There was no longer any person in a leadership position acting for and on behalf of what had been the centre. There was no agenda, vision, plan, or king to direct the life of any saint or sinner who decided to walk through the door. The meeting was over and the gathering had begun. It was as if we could now look around the room and see each other. Those of us who were there had made a choice to be here and there we were. Being in church meetings for the 25 years I had been a Christian, I knew that this morning was different. It was not outwardly strong, but its reality was stronger than I had ever felt. The gathering now was a composite of those who were there and no longer something constructed by a platonic mirage of mirrors. It was the weakest strongest thing on earth. It was simply and profoundly his body the church gathered in a room to be who we were.

An offer too good not to refuse

A few days after this one of the elders who had walked the journey of transition was playing his guitar at home. He suddenly felt a strong counsel activated inside his mind that in effect said: 'You can lead this people. You can care for them, love them and take them into strength.' For a moment he felt drawn to such a persuasive leadership offer. Then he shook himself and with a few words dispatched the headhunter from his mind. After that there was no one in a position of influence who could be influenced by such an offer. The centre had no support, the generational strongholds had no footing, the Nicolaitan could no longer draw blood to keep it going, the fallen angels had no occasion to look in any longer. The death was complete and in that instant the life was known like never before – life to the gathering and life to the culture this gathering helped to express, resource and intensify.

I am getting nervous now about the extent of autobiographical content here, but while we are here we may as well complete the diary entry. Soon after this breakthrough I moved with my family to the United Kingdom for six months and then returned to see our Pentecostal fellowship join with a Methodist one. This blend had much providence, far too much to go into here, but it was very evident to many that God's purposes were in it. We had been preparing for this during the time of transition and at times people would say: Why are you joining with a traditional congregation if you are so enthusiastic to press in to a more radical future oriented one? My reply drew from the good steward who brings forth out of his treasure things both old and new. The wells and the covenants, the promises and prayers made by saints of old are very real and must be carried into the new. The streams that carry these histories in the present have much to contribute to the new. Those who dislodge from their good heritage might think they are on the cutting edge, but they are not. That edge, that point of the spear, can only thrust into the future if it has the shaft and weight of history behind it.

If your spirit is free then, as you press into the good, even though you will labour with the power structures, you will not have to come under their jurisdiction. Thus, you can do business with the settings in which they are found and, generally, see them overcome. In this coming together we did not simply join two congregations of different persuasions. To do so would be a problem, if not a disaster. Instead, with the freedom we had won we moved both fellowships into a new expression of the gathering that focused on the best of both traditions and on the life and work of the people as the church in all of life. None of this was (or is) ideal, however it was (and is) very real and enjoyable. Three years on there has now been a generational handover, which we, and many looking on, find remarkable.

Again, each person and place will track a different, but related journey into the new. We have not looked at the development of the 'out there' culture in which the church as fullness arises. A treatment of the contours of this new landscape, including elements such as building the culture, the nature and function of leadership, ways of gatherings and so on are covered in a book I have written with David Oliver (UK) called *Church that Works* (Word UK). Suffice to say that in my experience the more that the church as construct went into death the more the momentum in the new landscape increased. As people were released from the church as construct they naturally began to experience more of what it was to be the church as fullness.

As leaders we have the double blessing of bringing the saints to maturity, to the measure of the stature that belongs to the fullness of Christ. It is in the all things of creation that this growth occurs. As such, ministry is not primarily about congregation growth; it's about the church as fullness. Our only hope in seeing our gatherings enriched and growing will be to see the saints we minister to enriched and growing in life. This is what Jesus came and died for, and this is what we must now die to see arise. Sixteen hundred years under platonic influence is a long time for us, but it's only a day and a half in the sight of God. Let's get his sight, let's die his death and let's go after his life in, through and over all things.

Chapter 16

No Centre Please, We're Saints

Much of this book has been about the nature and use of authority. That being the case, it is good to return to that subject once again before we close. This will necessitate somewhat of a Bible study. You might think that after all of your hard work in reading through a book like this you would have deserved something more resounding than a Bible study. In my defence I call to the stand idealism and his criminal-mate consumerism. I rest my case for such an anticlimactic outro on the hope that by not giving closure, idealism, methodology or guarantees to the readers I will encourage them to seek the highlights and the fullness encouraged in this book in their own life and inheritance in creation.

Here we want to look at the teaching of Scripture with regard to the nature and function of authority in the light of our understanding of the church as fullness. What might authority look and act like if it were dispersed from the collapsed house and seeded into the body of Christ standing in and through creation? As this study proceeds you may well find it difficult to get a handle on what scriptural leadership in fact is. This lack of clarity is intentional, both on my part with regard to the study and, I believe, on the part of God in his communication on the matter. Authority should not be fixed, central and owned; rather, God intends it to be integrated, fluid and dispersed among his people. For this reason it is easier to discover what authority should not be than to work out what it is meant to be – that being said, there are, of course, many important perspectives on the nature and function of authority that can be gleaned from Scripture. As we shall see, these gleanings make much more sense when we look at them from the vantage point of the church as fullness. Before we proceed let's engage in one more review of the ground we have covered.

We have looked at the reasons why Western society is so prone to constructing institutions that take up a central role over people and process. In particular, we have noted the use of platonic dualism and idealism in the formulation of the thinking and, from there, the structures that create these centrist edifices. The record of history shows that whenever the elements and the people that make for the church of Jesus Christ are brought together in and under one person (or one group) then a power structure, which is Nicolaitan, forms over people and process. Whenever the elements that make for the church of God are collapsed together in one house and come under the control of one person – with the culture, resources, ministry initiatives and gatherings coming under that rule – then dysfunction sets in. It is this centrist obsession, with the dualism and idealism that come with its platonic package, which binds the people of God to authority structures and prevents their full release into creation.

To overcome we need to firstly be aware of the power and strategy of the platonic agenda. Secondly we must be willing to go into the dying of Jesus; this being a death to platonic strongholds in our own minds and a dying to the structures they have created. From there we need to embrace a way and vision of being church that moves beyond our present centrist-congregation/construct-focus into the creation. It is the Hebrew vision of the heavens and the earth that enables us to see the church as Christ's body standing in and growing up through the all things of the present creation. Once this body is seen, felt and known as *us*, then we can begin to place the various expressions of authority God has given us – leaders, elders, apostles and other ministry gifts – throughout that creation-encompassing vision and vista of church. With such an understanding in place we can begin to more effectively engage in a separation of powers to see good order, good culture and good works emerge in every sphere of creation. Let's now proceed to the promised Bible study.

The Bible study

Jesus told us that we should not be like the 'great men (who) exercise authority over' others. A telling phrase, one that comes on the back of the well known, don't be like the 'rulers of the Gentiles (who) lord it over' people (Mt. 20:25). Is Jesus saying we should not exercise any authority over people? It would appear so. One might say in response to this that 'we can exercise authority over people, as long as we don't do it like the dictators do'. Perhaps, but I would think that this is letting us off the hook far too easily. It would seem to me that Jesus was talking about a much more radical approach to authority than 'you can trust me, I am not a dictator, I am a church leader. My rule, as distinct from others, is for the people, it's for their good . . . and so on.'

Certainly leaders do have an authority from God that people should submit and respond to. However, before we as leaders jump over that statement on our way to the executive chair, we need to stop and define the 'authority' and the 'submit' parts of that statement. The first thing I would say is that New Testament leadership is never exercised *over* the church; rather, it is carried out *in relation* to it. Leaders were never given the right to take up a managerial role over the church process. As overseers they were called to 'take care of the church' (1 Tim. 3:5) and did this by 'keeping watch over [people's] soul' (Heb. 13:17). What this means is that overseers sit, like elders, in the gates of a city of old, and guard the environment of the city in which the church exists and grows. They work to ensure that the atmosphere of that city is good and conducive to the growth of those within its walls. This does involve times of intervention for discipline, justice or defence against attack, but such will be intermittent, as the need arises, rather than a continuous exertion of leadership over people and process. The book of Judges speaks of this kind of leadership with regard to Gideon, a man raised up for a season to deliver Israel from its enemies. When the battle was fought and won Gideon, desiring to resume normal life as God had intended, said to his brethren, 'I will not rule over you, nor shall my son rule over you; the Lord shall rule over you' (Judg. 8:23). That being said, the people still took a hold of the warrior's vest, made from the gold and jewels given to him after his victory, and 'played the harlot with it . . . so that it became a snare to Gideon and his household' (Judg. 8:27). Leadership is a dangerous game, is it not?

This exercise of 'alongside authority' is a world away from the rule of the monarch. The elders sit around the city caring for and watching over it. The monarch sits at the centre ruling and directing it. The King James Version is alone among the major translations in its description of leaders as those who 'have the rule over you' (Heb. 13:17). Besides not being supported by the Greek text, it also contradicts the teaching of Jesus concerning the lords and great men who 'rule over' people. Further to this we note that when leaders are referred to in various passages their function rather than their role is emphasised in the description. In the verse from Hebrews quoted above we read (following the phrasing in the Greek), of 'the ones leading you' and in 1 Timothy 5:17 we hear of the 'well-ruling elders'. It was the process or the work of leaders that was in view rather than the focus being on their positional authority. Such an understanding of God's way of leadership is hard to convey because we are so accustomed to it being defined positionally, rather than functionally – hence Jesus' teaching concerning lords and great men who rule over people and his attempt to get believers to see leadership as a servant task rather than a leadership position.

Do the leaders/elders/overseers (whatever we might choose to call them) have authority? Is it positional? My answer would be yes, on both counts. Again, I would argue that the position is still functional rather than fixed, and the authority exercised is not constant and 'over', but intermittent and alongside. One might say that a plumber has a position (as a plumber) and an authority in relation to the jobs that are given him. When things go wrong it is best to submit to his vocation and expertise in the matter. However, the pipes in your house do not belong to the plumber once the job is done. They do not come under his continuous jurisdiction, to do with as he pleases. A response to this might be that we have no right to decide who our elders are, as we do a plumber. My first response is that, more often that not, we do in fact choose our elders, rather than them choosing us – a good thing, I believe. I might add another example that some may think better fits the bill. When you are obeying the law and sitting at home with your family the police have no right to come into your house and tell you to turn off the lights and all go to bed. If they do then they are moving outside of their jurisdiction. If, however, there was a criminal in your home, and, say it was you, then the police would have the right to come in and exercise their authority by taking you away before the courts. Authority and position exist, but they are only valid when exercised within their given jurisdiction.

The term 'well-ruling elders' that I quoted from 1 Timothy 5:17 informs us of this functional, rather than positional role that leaders have. The word 'ruling' used here by Paul is not the Greek noun for ruler (*archēgos*); rather, it is a participle that speaks of a person going before, or travelling in advance of another (*proestōtes*). This reference is the only time that the word 'rule' is used in Scripture regarding those in positions of authority in the church. It suggests a way of life that sets an example for others to follow. It does not speak of elders occupying positions that enable them to exercise power over others. We might be well served to say that elders do not have the *position* of leadership *over* the church; rather, they have a *place* of leadership *in* the church.

So it is with every other 'place' given to people within the body of Christ. Each one has an authority in line with their gifting, their willingness to serve and their created desires for goodness. In this line-up of giftings and places 1 Corinthians 12:28 speaks of apostles being appointed first in the church. Should you feel the need to apply for the position, the job description for those who are first is given in 1 Corinthians 4:9–13! Again, what is in view in this first place is function more than position. These people are called, like Paul, to break new ground and commence the kingdom-building process in a new city or region. Peter, the apostle, was given the right to open the door of faith to first the Jews and then the Gentiles. It is because they are 'first' that they can establish a track and a tradition for others to respond to and travel upon.

The only times Paul asserted his authority as an apostle was when he was being challenged by those who were seeking to dominate the church. The best example of this is when the so-called super apostles tried to deceive the Corinthian saints. Even here the way he defended his calling as an apostle was rather strange! He played the suffering fool to win his case over those who set out to 'enslave', 'devour', 'take advantage' and 'exalt' themselves over the saints (2 Cor. 11:20). It needs to be said here that Paul was not defending any right on his part to leadership authority over the church of Corinth. Rather, he was defending his role as initiator and father to the church in that city, over and against those who were endeavouring to take control of the centre.

Another point in passing here: it seems that Paul, in matters of discipline, wanted the church as community to itself enact discipline. In the Corinthian situation he did not address elders in the matter of discipline (1 Cor. 5:1–7). This is not to say that elders did not exist or were not important to the church in Corinth. Perhaps it was because of the struggle with super apostles that their role was being compromised. Whichever way, Paul saw the gathered church as having an authority to act in discipline, thus pointing the way to where he saw divine authority in the church residing. Paul's decision to hand the offender over to Satan, that is, casting him out of fellowship, seemed to be precipitated because the church gathered had failed to act as it should have in the matter. Paul's authority only came in because the community of the church failed to act when they should have. Intervention by elders was not the first port of call, but was instead a backup, one that served to initiate a discipline process that had failed.

We see this progression in Matthew 18:15. Jesus said that if one person wrongs another then the matter should first be dealt with privately between the offender and the one offended. Then, if that fails, two or more are brought in to look at the matter. Finally, if the issue is not resolved then it is carried before a more representative gathering of the church. Again, elders are not mentioned here, but that is not to say that Jesus did not foresee their role. The point here is that the authority rests among the people. As such, elders need to act in relation to that authority in a representative role and intermittent way, as the need arises.

Jesus tells us in Matthew 23:8–12

> Do not be called Rabbi; for one is your teacher, and you are all brothers. And do not call anyone on earth your father; for one is your Father, he who is in heaven. And do not be called leaders; for one is your leader, that is, Christ. But the greatest among you shall be your servant. And whoever exalts himself shall be humbled; and whoever humbles himself shall be exalted.

The words 'rabbi', 'father' and 'leader' have the definite article 'the' before them when used of Christ or the Father. Quite clearly this means that we can have people who function as teachers or overseers but we should have no one person (or construct) that operates as a fixed central reference point for truth and authority. By way of contrast with the sitting-alongside-the-city blueprint for elders, let's now look at what Scripture says about the rule of the people process from the centre.

The idol/ideal king

The king thing, as mentioned, came in because Israel was not happy with having only elders, judges and prophets working to establish and maintain good order in the nation. They were particularly unhappy about having an invisible God as their king and ruler and instead wanted a visible man they could identify with. So a man they got. He made a centre and the rest is history – sad but true. Telling were the words of God on that day that Israel rejected his rule over them. The king, he said, will

'take your sons and place them for himself in his chariots and among his horsemen and they will run before his chariots. And he will appoint for himself commanders of thousands and of fifties, and some to do his ploughing and to reap his harvest and to make his weapons of war and equipment for his chariots. He will also take your daughters for perfumers and cooks and bakers. And he will take the best of your fields and your vineyards and your olive groves, and give them to his servants. And he will take a tenth of your seed and of your vineyards, and give to his officers and to his servants. He will also take your male servants and your female servants and your best young men and your donkeys, and use them for his work. He will take a tenth of your flocks, and you yourselves will become his servants. Then you will cry out in that day because of your king whom you have chosen for yourselves, but the LORD will not answer you in that day.' Nevertheless, the people refused to listen to the voice of Samuel, and they said, 'No, but there shall be a king over us, that we also may be like all the nations, that our king may judge us and go out before us and fight our battles' (1 Sam. 8:12–20).

These words act as their own commentary on the matter of central rule. Is it any wonder Jesus did not want the church to be ruled over by lords or great men? In summary of what we have covered thus far we can, I believe, state that the difference between elders and rulers is that elders sit at the gates around the city to care for and watch over it, whereas rulers sit at the centre of a process and a people to rule over and control them. Jesus never intended that authority accumulate in one place and in one person. For those who might be tempted to think that authority in the local church is categorically different from authority in the realm of government, think again. Jesus seemed to think that the pitfalls that rulers of nations were prone to, the leaders of the church could easily follow.

Magnets among iron filings

Many leaders would agree with what I have said thus far in regards to leadership and authority. The challenge is that for the most part they are unable to put it into practice in their church. Pastors start out in ministry endeavouring to do what it takes to mobilise people for their own ministry out there in the world. Years later, however, they wake up to find they are the business manager of a congregation, employed to direct the church people and church process from the centre. As the years spin by they find it near impossible to overcome the centrifugal force ever moving them to rule (or more politely, manage) the centre. The greatest obstacle to authority working as God intended it to work is that it tries to function in a setting God did not design it for. Authority sets up shop inside a construct designed in accordance with platonic dualism and idealism and, as such, is ever drawn to the centre of that construct to rule. The platonic agenda ensures that authority does not, because it cannot, ultimately serve the body as God intended. Again, it is only as we place that God-given authority in the church as fullness that the separation of powers will break the hold of the centre and work in an ongoing way to ensure that the authority elements do not coagulate in a centre again. Leadership, elders, ministry gifts and deacons are too powerful to live in close proximity to each other. They need the city or region to move and function in. They need the body, living and working in every sphere of creation, to keep them busy, keep them serving, keep them from becoming entangled in the affairs of everyday church-as-construct business.

Elders are called to work to bring about an environment that promotes the growth of the body in all things. As such they do not (and indeed cannot) encompass the breadth and diversity of the many good works of the saints in every sphere of life under some management grid. Good eldering in a city or region is able to encourage a far more fluid, spacious and multi-faceted culture of church into being. It facilitates an environment where Christ's body the church can grow in health, in business, in the arts and media, in education, in the family and so on. It can serve a city-wide process that enables the body to gather in many and varied ways in relationship with ministry gifts who, together with elders, encourage and equip them the saints for their own works of ministry. This way of authority does not diminish leadership; to the contrary it draws out its divine purpose all the more, which brings great benefit to the body and the leaders who are part of that body.

This kind of authority is such as to make submission and obedience to leaders easy. The Bible says we are called to be 'subject to one another' (Eph. 5:21). This way of life calls us to respond to one another – as husband and wife, elder and saint, giver and receiver – a long time before obedience becomes an issue. The more we take the initiative and respond, the less we have to obey. It is this kind of relationship of which I believe the Scripture speaks. It is this kind of relationship that God himself desires to have with each of us as his sons and daughters. When authority is exercised as needed and then is able to go quiet and retire to the gates then people will have a greater desire and trust when it comes to responding to it. There are too many saints on the run from overmuch eldering. If elders sought less control, if church leaders lost that hungry look when spying a potential new member coming through the door, they will find that, over time, people will respond more to their leadership, not less.

Submission was never meant to be about one losing one's rights to personhood. It is God's way to bring us into relationship with others, with those whose gifts we need to complete our life as one body standing in creation. When we submit to another we respond to who they are and what they desire to give. Leaders are not the only people we are meant to submit to. We are meant to submit, appropriately, to every person desiring to give good things to us. This way of life multiplies the attributes, nature and power in valid authority down the line into life, rather than constipating it in a central position or office. In the new landscape there will not be less leadership and authority, there needs to be more, much more, of the right kind of it. Let's now look at some of the issues relating to authority handover.

From corporate managers to the generational fathers

A major part of our problem with authority transference arises from the way in which platonic (dis)reality has caused us to create constructs that house and hold power over people and process. This brings a situation where, after many years, there exists a whole lot of 'somethings' that need to be passed on to somebody. The construct has now got assets, a brand name, a following and so on, which, of necessity, need to be handed over. Much of our problem with the stewardship issues here relates to the problem we ourselves created in the first place. It is not enough to say well, we have all these assets so we just have to take care of them. We need to dig deeper and ask ourselves why we, as church leaders, accumulated them in the first place.

If from the start, or for the future, we had a vision of the church as fullness and the separation of powers therein, then much of this problem of handover would not arise;

this is because there would not be many assets and there would be no 'following' to have to hand over to another. If the people were permitted to own the works of ministry they do, yes, even the charitable works, then these (and the plant and equipment that accumulates from them) would not amass under one leader's wing and construct. It may be necessary at times for a building to be purchased in which to hold larger meetings. Once, however, we know we are the church and give ourselves the permission to meet in different ways and various settings, we will be able to see more and more gatherings happen in homes and businesses, as well as in these larger buildings.

The point I am making here is that the more we see the church as fullness in every sphere of life, the more we can gather as that church in all of life. This will mean less pressure on leaders to have and hold larger assets like buildings. I am not saying these are necessarily a problem and should all be sold. Rather, I am speaking here of the easing of pressure to have a church centre once the psychological centre is removed and the action is situated in all of life. The more we do this the more we will keep resources moving out into people's lives in creation and the less we will see assets making their way into the church centre.

God intended a situation in Israel where power and wealth would not accumulate in the centre, but rather travel down lines of the generations and into the nations to bless them. The Jubilee, though never followed, is always a tantalising option for the brave of heart. From time to time to disperse power by forgiving debt and returning land accumulated over the years to families in need, families God gave the land to in the first place, is something that we will not do because of our current approach to power. It is telling to see whole or half of certain islands in the South Pacific now owned and unused by the church, with indigenous people in need of land not given the right to even occupy or use that land. What was meant to bless ends up controlling time and time again. This hard option for the handover of the assets and the dispersing of the authority associated with ownership of those assets is one that needs to be mentioned here. The young man who asked Jesus what he must do to inherit eternal life received a strong dose of the above wisdom in answer. He was told to sell all and give it away to those in need. We need to be willing to taste the same. Imagine the influence one might gain if one was willing to give away power.

Three generations and you're out

God brought into place after the Fall an aging and dying process. Intrinsic in this is a way of handover of authority from one generation to another. In the creation reality God intended that people emerge from family and be released by their fathers (and mothers) into creation. God is first described as the God of Abraham, Isaac and Jacob. As the three-generational God, he purposed there be a relationship between the generations that established the breadth and depth of life and heritage that would serve the divine purpose. God intends that sons and daughters prophesy, young men see the vision and old men dream dreams (Joel 2:28). The progression is obvious. In youth we are given the capacity to prophesy into the new and press into the cutting edge of what God is bringing to the fore. As we become fathers/parents we see the vision for our life come into focus through our good work. Then, as we grow old and our vigour starts to fade, we begin to dream the dreams of wisdom and can no longer hang on to the main game as we once did. We are forced, as it were, by our years and by the vigour of the emerging generations to release more and more of the initiative and the work to them. This is a hard time for any father of fathers. Finally, there comes a time when we will die and our inheritance – the traditions, resources and collective memory – will be fully given over to the generations that follow. The father's inheritance is dispersed among the generations in this way.

The way life is in the fallen state is such that authority cannot be held onto. Life makes sure that those with authority and power must give way over time to the up and coming generations. This God-ordained way of dispersal of authority is countered by the platonic agenda in its setting up and rule of the state or the institution. The construct or company, as distinct from real humans, is, in the Western mind, deemed to be alive and, as long as no one closes it down, it can live (and rule) forever. This means that church constructs or denominations function like companies and not like families. One might say that the difference between a company and a family is that a company seeks servants to produce its product, whereas a father desires to have sons to release into their inheritance in creation.

The rule of the company sets up a scenario whereby assets and people are joined to, and thus owned or managed by, the construct. This means that the authority, heritage and resource that are to be dispersed down the generational lines are kept in the hands of the company and its managers. A person cannot hold on and must die. A company holds on and never dies. Hence the need for those in leadership to die to the construct, release the elements therein and radically redefine their relationship to the church as fullness. No longer can they be managers of the church central. They need to become servants of the church as fullness.

When the construct is no more and a culture of release and generational handover becomes normative, then the sons and daughters will no longer have to continually engage in the killing (blood letting) process that so often occurs when one era or generation gives way to the next. So much blessing, resource and cultural memory is wasted as the construct accumulates wealth, becomes brittle and then dies under the weight of its own judgement. Power is never good if it is kept and accumulated. It is only good if it is given away, dispersed and released into life. If we no longer had platonic centres built on the plain of life, trying, Babel-like, to short cut the process to the heavens, then we would no longer have to regularly die to them, or be killed by them. We would no longer have to deal with constructs that dislocate the inheritance of the fathers from the life of the sons and daughters. Rather, we would see a natural dying process in action, one that continually bequeaths life, blessing and wisdom down the lines of the generations. Each of us has immense authority. We have been trained in dependence too long. We have power, gifting, desire, permission and responsibility to occupy the life before us. Let's keep multiplying the power we have been given by continually giving it away.

Mother, how quickly will the future come?

One person said to me recently, 'We taught them they were the church; we ordained them for their work and sphere of influence and released them to go for it. Here we are six months later and nothing has happened. People are starting to ask what is going on, what's happening, what have we done wrong?' We have been so programmed for fireworks on a short wick, lit at the climax of meetings and conference, going off with great noise and colour to create that 'WHAAA!' response; a response over in a flash and not taken home. This time is not that time; this is the time when the leaven silently makes its way through the lump.

This is a time for a person to sow the seed in the ground and go to sleep (very non-managerial) and then wake up in the morning and be amazed that the seed had the capacity to grow of itself (Mk. 4:27). A watched pot is like a watched seed and very unlike a watched fireworks display.

It takes time for those born and bred on idealism to come down from their addiction and begin to settle into the life of the good, relational, normal and hard. Saints have, of course, been doing this to their own life for many years. However, for many their church life has been a safe, ideal and otherworld experience that has not affected them in the same way that normal life has. When the church becomes us and the gathering and the fullness are one seamless garment, this divide will be gone and the protection from reality that the ecclesiastic shell has given will be no more. Saints in this new landscape will feel their lack and this loss for a time before they begin to sense and know their good desire rising. Even when that desire first rises it will not meet the fruit of good work; rather, it will meet thorns that will speak more to the saint about themselves than they have known before. Before the anticipated life and fruit is tasted, a death will come. Life and fruit they could not have anticipated will rise from this death. It will take time for the righteous angels of the second heaven to become convinced that we are serious about our occupation of the heavens. They have heard our brave pulpit proclamations come to naught in the face of popular lack of support from the business-as-usual lobby too many times before to jump quickly. Only as we live the life and work the works will they garrison and establish all that is real and good in what we do in the atmospheres over the city.

One might ask, how long till we reach the fullness? The question and its answer are really a non-issue. If we fix our sights on some future goal (unless of course that goal is more of Jesus), then we will tend to not pay enough attention to the people and the process as it unfolds. Or worse, we will make a rod from our ideal goal and use it to drive the people and the process in line with our vision of the way things should be. We cannot allow ideal arrival points to dictate the process of development towards the fullness. We must learn to look to the good that arises from the desire of hearts. It is in relationship with each other, with creation and with God the creator that more than enough good work will rise to light our way into more of the good.

One might ask, how long will it take for the old to die and the new culture to become established? I don't know the answer to either part of that question. What I do know is that as soon as two or more agree on any one thing, there they have Christ in their midst. As soon as two or more decide to do a good work together, the power of agreement from heaven is theirs and the new culture between them has begun. One does not need to wonder when 'the church' will get its act together and change. Such a comment is often simply used as an excuse to not take responsibility individually as a member of Christ's body, the church. We do not need to wait for the church at large to get *it*, any more than we need to wait for every family on earth to become functional before our family decides to stop being dysfunctional. You begin to live and let the rest of life catch up.

In the new landscape church we do not need managers and we do not need a centre. We can afford to have commentators identifying this and that. We can welcome elders to watch and care for the new and large spaces opening up before the sons and daughters. And we can call forth the ministry gifts to help equip the church as fullness to occupy those spaces in every sphere of creation. However, let the visionaries know that they see in part, let the prophets be aware that they prophesy in part and if any leader comes and tells us he or she knows the future, then let them purchase a dim mirror (1 Cor. 13:12) and look again. For now let's embrace death and begin to breathe the life its travail brings our way.

Further Reading

BANA, G., *The Second Coming of the Church: A blueprint for survival* (Nashville: Word, 1998)

KIRKPATRICK, C., M. PIERSON and M. RIDDELL, *The Prodigal Project* (London: SPCK, 2000)

MARSHALL, T., *Understanding Leadership* (Chichester: Sovereign World, 1991)

MITCHELL, R. and S., *Target Europe* (Chichester: Sovereign World, 2001)

OLIVER, D. and J. THWAITES, *Church that Works* (Milton Keynes: Word, 2001)

POPPER, K., *The Open Society and its Enemies. Volume 1. The spell of Plato* (London: Routledge, 1966 [1989])

SCOTT, M., *Sowing Seeds for Revival* (Chichester: Sovereign World, 2001)

THWAITES, J., *The Church Beyond the Congregation: The strategic role of the church in the postmodern era* (Carlisle: Paternoster, 1999)

WINK, W., *Engaging the Powers* (Minneapolis: Fortress, 1992)

Glossary of words and terms

'Church as construct' – refers to a church fellowship that perceives itself to be a distinct organisation – so much so that the church becomes a discrete and separate entity in peoples' thinking, belief and behaviour.

'Church as fullness' – a phrase drawn from Ephesians 1:23. It refers to the church that exists in all of life and work, growing up in every sphere of creation (marriage, family and work) to the heavens over the earth. A vision of the church drawn from the Hebrew worldview.

'Church as household' – a phrase drawn from 1 Timothy 3:15 that refers to the church gathered in various places and at various times. This expression of the church is called to be the pillar and support (the servant) to the church that exists in all of life and work in creation.

'Counsels' – in the context in which this word is used it refers to arguments, reasons, refutations directed against someone who questions the validity of a power structure.

'Dualism' – a worldview, particularly found in Platonic thinking, that says that the present material and relational creation exists as something distinct and separate from the divine and spiritual realm. It divides spiritual from material, sacred from secular, heaven from earth and so on. In this way it describes our life in creation mostly in negative terms, it divides our thinking, hinders our ability to experience God in all of life and leaves us prone to be dominated by those in power.

'Elemental things' – A term drawn from Galatians 4:3 and 4:9. It refers to the instinctual or basic elements of life – desire for food, sexual expression and other appetites basic to our nature. These things are created by God to serve us in life, but we can come under their control and end up serving them.

'Generational strongholds' – ways of thinking and believing over many years or centuries that form the culture of a people group or sphere of work. It represents the amalgamation of many individual strongholds over a long period of time. Such a process can of course happen for the good or the bad, the emphasis here, in line with the definition of stronghold from 2 Corinthians 10:4f, is towards the downside affect.

'Gordian Knot' – a term from the Greek legends. It was an intricate and complicated knot that no one could untie, but was, supposedly, cut by the sword of Alexander the Great. Indicates a problem for which there appears to be no solution.

'Idealism' – an aspect of Platonic thinking drawn from dualism. Platonic thinking causes us to think that there exists an ideal thing or place outside of our human experience, one that is perfect, spiritual and divine. This causes us to think that our present experience of life holds little or no substance and that only some ideal future or ideal thing will be able to define and give meaning to our lives.

'Immanence' – the expression of God's person and presence that we can experience within this finite creation.

'Transcendence' – the expression of God's infinite person and presence existing beyond the finite creation outside of our capacity to experience.

'Ministry Gifts' – A term drawn from Ephesians 4:7-12. The list given there includes apostles, prophets, evangelists, pastors and teachers. These persons are an actual gift of Christ to the body – thus the emphasis is not so much on their giftedness, but on the fact that they are a gift to others. The reason why they are given is listed in verse 12 onwards – the first of these is to equip the saints for the work of ministry (service, works in creation) – hence the term ministry gift.

'Strongholds' – refers to a fortress that defends a position against attack or overthrow. Drawn from 2 Corinthians 10:4,5. Strongholds are ways of thinking (speculation, knowledge, 'lofty things') that are 'raised up against the knowledge of God'. They are beliefs that resist the purpose of God in ones' life.

'New Landscape Church' – a phrase that describes a way of being church that has the creation rather than the congregation as its primary context. If we are under the influence of platonic thinking we tend to focus more on a removed spiritual and ideal realm rather than the physical and relational creation. When we come to understand that the body of Christ is called to grow up in all things of the present creation to the heavens of God over the earth, then the earth itself (land, society, spheres of creation) comes into focus as the primary place for our works of service in God. Our calling is to dwell in and work the land/earth before us, landscaping it in such a way that it becomes an expression of who we are as people created in God's image.

'Nicolaitan' – A term drawn from Revelation 2:6,15. It is a composite word made up of the Greek words Nican – to rule or conquer, and Laos – meaning people. It is not certain what this term precisely means, but the context in which it is placed suggests a way of exercising authority that brings people under the bondage and control of others. Nicolaitan is the Greek word for the 'Balaam' – an Old Testament character. Hence the connecting word 'thus' found in Revelations 2:15 following on from the comment on Balaam in the previous verse.

'Power Structures' – These are human institutions that derive their power by making use of generational strongholds. A society or culture calls for and gets the kind of leadership that lines up with its beliefs concerning life (as in, you get the leaders you deserve). Power structures can arise in response to peoples' aspirations and can also come into a position of control by taking undue advantage of the weaknesses created by strongholds in peoples' thinking. Often, of course, it is taken on the basis of a mixture of the two.

'Principalities and Powers' – a phrase drawn from Ephesians 6:12 (KJV) and Romans 8:38 (NASB). Fallen angelic beings that oversee territory (principalities) and spheres of creation (powers). As angels they were initially created to back up and serve human reality. In the fallen state they derive most of their power to influence the 'atmospheres' over the earth from human power structures.

'Third Heaven' – Term drawn from 2 Corinthians 12:2. In line with the Hebrew worldview the created order is made up of three heavens existing over the earth. The first heavens are the realm of humanity, the second is the realm of angels and the third is the heaven of God, where his throne is manifest to and over the creation. Each of these heavens interact and interpenetrate. Paul speaks of the Gospel being proclaimed in all of creation under heaven (Col. 1:23). Strictly speaking the third heaven of God is distinct from the angelic and human heavens in that it was not affected by the Fall in Adam. It still, however, exists in relation to the earth and now, because of the incarnation, is open once again to those who are in Christ.

'Thorns over creation's fullness' – Many think that at the time of divine judgement after the Fall of Adam the creation was written off and now only waits to be destroyed by fire. In line with the Hebrew worldview we understand that at the time of the Fall creation's fullness (the full measure of its good) was rendered inaccessible to humanity by God. Its fullness was hidden behind the thorns, the sweat, the futility (Rom. 8:20ff) and ultimately because of human death could never be reached. These thorns are the hard places in creation. They are a reality sign that reveal to us the true state of our fallenness and dislocation from life in God. When Jesus Christ came he suffered his way through the judgements of the Fall and has once again made a way through them into the fullness of creation and the heavens over creation. We are now called to 'suffer with him'

(Rom. 8:17) and go through the hard places of life to see change come to our lives, engaging the creation to see its fullness and our inheritance emerge. Note: A more detailed treatment of this can be found in Chapter 11 of *The Church Beyond the Congregation.*